What others are saying…

"In my twenty years of service with the International Mission Board, I do not know of another missionary in the country of Brazil who has risked his life more for the advancement of the gospel than Eric Reese. God spared Eric's life on a number of occasions as he walked through the "Valley of the Shadow of Death" in the dangerous slums of Rio de Janeiro."

- **Keith E. Jefferson**, International Mission Board Emeritus Missionary to Brazil, former Strategy Coordinator of the people group, Quilombolas.

"From a short-term mission trip to a lifetime of mission service, Eric Reese, tells his story. It is the story that takes the reader from the racially troubled and poverty-stricken U.S. Deep South to ministry in the dangerous favelas of Rio de Janeiro, Brazil. It is a story of protective prayer and transforming power.

Fellow missionaries, especially those who serve in dangerous places, will read this book with understanding, and draw from its pages, strength to continue their task. Non-missionaries will read this book with appreciation and find themselves praying even more for those on the front lines of challenging ministry.

Some will even read this book with a fresh understanding of God's call on their lives to further mission involvement. All who read this book will be blessed, as well as challenged."

- **Dr. Dan R. Crawford**, Senior Professor of Evangelism & Missions, Chair of Prayer Emeritus, Southwestern Baptist Seminary, Fort Worth, Texas.

"Many missionaries obediently follow God's call to places their lives may be in danger. It is not always because of hostility to a Christian witness as much as crime and anarchy, ethnic conflict, disease, or natural disasters in a world that does not know Jesus.

However, in this book, Eric Reese describes intentionally embracing the fears and dangers of taking the gospel to the slums of Rio de Janeiro, Brazil in a fascinating testimony of God's protection and faithfulness. In a no man's land of poverty, disease and crime ruled by drug lords and marked by frequent gun battles, Eric testifies to the power of the gospel to transform lives and communities.

You will find your heart beating faster and adrenaline rushing as you read of constant life-threatening encounters, but your emotions will overflow as you read of God's deliverance and grace."

- **Jerry Rankin**, President Emeritus, International Mission Board, SBC

"The life devotion along with God's call on Eric Reese life has produced a miraculous work that's motivated by the Cross. Read how this servant made an eternal difference in one of the world's largest and most dangerous cities. Your faith will be inspired, and your commitment challenged."

- **Dr. Johnny Hunt**, Senior Vice President of Evangelism and Leadership - North American Mission Board

"Riveting! Absolutely riveting! This book is a life changer. Eric Reese is an incredible man with an unbelievable ministry and an unparalleled message. The gospel of Jesus Christ is true, and it works. This work again makes that abundantly clear. I cannot commend this book highly enough. It will bless and encourage all who read it."

- **Daniel L. Akin,** President, Southeastern Baptist Theology Seminary

"I have known Eric for 26 years and always admired his commitment to the ministry and his faithful service to our Lord Jesus Christ.

In this book Eric Reese takes you on a journey of his missionary experiences in the Favelas of Rio de Janeiro. If you are considering becoming a missionary this book gives insight into the highs and lows of life as a missionary. The book recounts many hair-raising experiences as well as the effects on his wife and children."

- **Jim McBride**, Executive Pastor, Sherwood Baptist Church Albany, Georgia

"Some authors are challenged when it comes to writing about life's experiences in a manner that captures the heart of the reader. Eric Reese has precisely the opposite difficulty. How can you wrap the cover of a book around a life that has been so adventurous, bold, and challenging for any advocate of the Gospel?

This book is bound to bring the reader to the humble admission that God has a place in His harvest for every believer in Christ."

- **Tom Elliff,** President Emeritus International Mission Board, Southern Baptist Convention

"Eric Reese is a modern missionary hero. Together with his wife, Ramona , daughters Gloria and Alicia, the Reese family has served the Lord in the concrete jungles of Rio de Janeiro and Sao Paulo , Brazil for the last quarter century.

Like missionary pioneers such as the William Carey's and the Adoniram Judson's, the Reese family has risked their lives in dangerous places on the mission field. While meeting human needs whenever possible, Eric has focused on proclaiming the Gospel of the cross of the risen Christ. Anyone interested in God's story of redeeming His world will be encouraged and inspired by this book.

The Reese family embodies the concept of giving one's life to serve in missions."

- **Robin Dale Hadaway,** Senior Professor of Missions- Midwestern Baptist Theological Seminary

"Only God's power and love poured out upon them and through them, can explain how Eric and Ramona managed not only to survive their many years of 'combat' with the forces of evil but indeed to 'free the oppressed' in so many wonderful ways dur- that time."

- **Fred Broome,** Retired Naval Officer

"This book will energize your faith in ways you cannot expect. Eric Reese's on-the-ground accounts of terrifying situations, with prayer as his only armor, will move you to recognize the power of prayer. This is a testament to all missionaries who have brave menacing environments around the world to spread God's message."

- **Willie McLaurin**, Vice President for Great Commission Relations and Mobilization, Southern Baptist Convention Executive Committee

Willing To Risk It ALL

For His Name's Sake

Eric Reese

© Copyright 2021 by Eric Reese

All rights reserved. No part of this collection may be reproduced or transmitted in any form or by any means, electronic or mechanical, including photocopying and recording, or by any information storage and retrieval system, except in the case of brief quotations for use in articles and reviews, without written permission from the author.

The views expressed in this book are the author's and do not necessarily reflect those of the publisher.

7710-T Cherry Park Dr, Ste 224
Houston, TX 77095
713-766-4271

Cover design by: Lucas Ribeiro de Deus
lucasribeiro.studio@gmail.com

ISBN: 9781648304286

Contents

Foreword xi

Acknowledgments xiii

Prologue xvii

Chapter 1: I Must Make a Difference 1

Chapter 2: Sensing a Call 19

Chapter 3: Into the Ministry 33

Chapter 4: Saying Goodbye 53

Chapter 5: Welcome to Rio 65

Chapter 6: Sense of Urgency 81

Chapter 7: Loving the Unlovely 101

Chapter 8: Man of Peace 121

Chapter 9: Truthfully Speaking 143

Chapter 10: Fear as a Companion 157

Chapter 11: Relying on God's Sufficient Grace 177

Chapter 12: Faith Conquers Fear 195

Chapter 13: Anger that Motivates 209

Chapter 14: Love to Lead, Lead to Love 231

Chapter 15: 'No' Is My Friend.. 239

Chapter 16: Leave or Stay?... 257

Chapter 17: Hitting Home 273

Chapter 18: A Final Challenge.. 297

Foreword

One more book about Missions?

Before you and I give into the temptation of asking this question, we should first reconsider the theme of this work—*In the Face of Fear*. While concerning Missions, this personal reflection goes beyond the theoretical, conceptual, or methodological perspective that we often expect. It enters the private realm of the heart in life-or-death circumstances. And if it is a confrontation of fear, it is also a confrontation of danger. In short, this exploration invites us to take a journey of faith while face to face with fear, *but in the presence of Jesus*.

The character and tone of the reading leaves no doubt that we are witnessing the genuine account of a "missionary's experience," or conversely, a "missionary experience" that brings forth a rich display of the highly personal nature of its meaning.

Dr. Eric Reese highlights the trajectory of his missionary ministry, as developed in the dangerous *favelas* (slum communities) of the city of Rio de Janeiro, Brazil. Maintaining the truthfulness and integrity of the facts described, yet carefully preserving the privacy and security of any sources used, Dr. Reese wisely applies the principle of discretion, changing the name and location of the *favelas* as necessary, as well as the people involved in the narrative. In Dr. Reese's view, "the central message of the book is the extraordinary protective power of prayer and the transforming power of love in Christ."

Rare and few are those who have walked alongside Dr. Reese in his journeys through the *favelas*. Thus, while hardly any of us have been unable to witness these events first-hand, Dr. Reese anticipated this possibility. Clothing his narrative in emotion and spiritual reflection through the dramatic experiences that he and his family have lived, he brings us excitement and inspiration, enriching our lives with hope and motivation in the face of the challenges, obstacles, and even dangers to which we are also exposed in our own journeys, even if we are unaware of them!

My prayer is that this noble account will bless your heart, encouraging and urging you to experience in your life, what was promised in 2 Timothy 1:7, "For God gave us not a spirit of fear, but of power, love, and moderation."

Thanks for the journey, Pastor Eric Reese! God bless your family and your ministry in Brazil! God bless the reading of your book in the hearts and minds of all readers!

- **Pr. Dr. Fausto A. Vasconcelos,** Pastor, Liberdade Church, São Paulo. President, Brazilian Baptist Convention

Acknowledgments

There are many people I'm indebted to, and I'd like to thank them.

My wife, Ramona, has been exactly the right mate for me. I've never known anyone who prays as much as she does, maybe because being married to me keeps her on her knees. I love you, honey. I thank God for my sweet daughters, Gloria, and Alicia. They are model daughters. They have been flexible and passionate to be involved in ministry with their parents. I'm so proud of their spiritual growth. My wife and daughters put up with me and pray for me. They see me get hurt sometimes, but still support me. They don't overreact. They keep me balanced when I'm off. "Every perfect gift is from above" (James 1:17). I believe they are three gifts from God.

A special thanks goes to Jerry Rankin, former president of the International Mission Board. Jerry came to Southwestern Baptist Theological Seminary when I was a student and spoke about missions. When he asked for people to come up front for prayer, I ran to the stage. I told him I felt called to missions, but my wife didn't. He encouraged me that God would call both of us, and he believed God would greatly use me. Those words changed my life. Jerry has a heart for the lost, and I'm thankful for his leadership.

A couple of pastors have influenced my life. Michael Catt, Pastor Emeritus of Sherwood Baptist in Albany, Georgia, has been an example to me for over twenty-eight years as a man of integrity and convictions. He helped me to get back on track with God. With his personal attention, Michael motivated me to overcome my fears of being discriminated against because of my race. I will always be grateful to him.

Johnny Hunt, Senior Vice President of Evangelism and Leadership - North American Mission Board has encouraged me for over fifteen years. I've watched his passion for the lost and the ministry. He says, "Love God, love people. Serve God, serve people." I learned this from him. I'll never forget the time he spent with me in South America. I'm grateful for his kindness.

A big thank-you goes to my ministry team of Brazilian brothers and sisters in Christ. They are the ones who did the work of God with us. It took all of us to reach people in Rio with the gospel of Christ. This team has embraced Ramona and me and walked beside us in ministry.

Julian spent three months in the *favelas* with me taking notes while I told him much of my story, sometimes until the wee hours of the morning. A university kid, he stuck to the task while also ministering to Brazilians. Without him, we couldn't have done this project. Julian, now Dr. Julian Swanson, serves as a medical doctor in Houston, Texas.

I want to honor and thank Kim P. Davis for her many hours of dedication in creating a readable book out of my words. She put her life in danger when she came to Brazil. What a trip! After accompanying me one night on a dangerous journey into a favela, she commented: "How alive at night reigns the kingdom of darkness." I am thankful for all her advice. She has been more than a co-writer; she has been a sister. I'm thankful she encouraged me to publish my story. May this story, released after her untimely passing, impact churches and members for the Great Commission.

Dan Allen, former IMB employee was kind enough to see the potential of my story to be published. He is all about the kingdom of God, not himself, and he's patient to see something through. Most of all, I want to thank the Lord Jesus Christ, who has loved me unconditionally and has shown me grace beyond measure. I only have a story because of His story. Amen!

Prologue

The instructions were clear: Park my truck in front of the plaza, wear a tie, and carry a Bible, but do *not* bring a cell phone.

I exited my truck and began walking down the middle of the darkened street. The streetlights are frequently turned off in the drug lord-run communities. So, I utilized my military background to control my breathing and concentrate on everything around me to sense anything suspicious.

Someone was following me. Mindful to not make too quick of a move, I turned to discover a young man with a gun on his hip.

A sinking feeling swamped me as I suddenly realized that I hadn't brought a tie, or a Bible as instructed—and I *had* brought my cell phone!

"Uncle," a voice said from my right, addressing me with a common Brazilian term of respect, "are you a pastor?" Through the faint natural light of the night, I saw the figure of a man but could make out no details about him. I knew enough about weapons, though, to identify the AK-47 assault rifle in his hands.

"I am," I answered.

The man directed me to raise my hands. So, he could frisk me for a weapon or a hidden microphone.

"I didn't wear a tie, and I left my Bible at home," I told him as he approached. "And I brought my cell phone."

"Please forgive me," I added.

The man said nothing. Instead, he took my cell phone from me and handing it back to me in four pieces. Then he blindfolded me and led me on a long walk—at least ten minutes—as with my left hand on his right shoulder and taking short, measured steps, I passed through the drug world of the slums of Rio de Janeiro and down a flight of stairs to my appointment with a leader of the local drug cartel.

"Thank you for coming, Pastor," the man-in-charge said after my blindfold was removed. He was the number three guy, the manager of the operation, so to speak, and as the one seated behind the desk, he did not need to inform me that he ruled the room.

I nodded in answer to the man's greeting and surveyed the dimly lit basement. I counted seven others carrying guns. At least there were seven who I could see. And the room was stocked with weapons.

But there was more tension in the room than weapons.

The police had beaten the brother of one of the area drug lord's managers. The brother died in a hospital from his head wounds, igniting two weeks of shootings and killings between the enraged drug dealers and the police.

I had received a phone call a few hours earlier from the community manager asking for my help. It was the second such request that day. The police chief had previously called, and I declined his offer to intervene between the two sides. I only accepted the second request after much prayer by my wife and me and after consulting my leader, Dennis Blackman, in São Paulo.

The major drug lord, locked up in jail, had recommended the American missionary—me—be brought in to calm matters, and police officials agreed I might be of some help. But first, the people involved had to hear me speak, to learn my motive and how it fits in between the drug lords' and the police's conflicting agendas.

Managers speak little in the Brazilian drug world, and this one only motioned for me to begin talking. I set out to introduce my purpose while being intentional not to make more than a split second of eye contact with the manager. Extended eye contact would be received as challenging his authority.

My heart had been on an all-out dash since entering the basement—probably at 150-160 beats per minute—but as I began sharing the gospel, I had come to Rio to spread, I was overwhelmed by the awareness that the manager was not *the* authority in the room. God's power overcame that room. I sensed my heart rate back at normal.

As I talked, one of the men became noticeably agitated and paced around the room. His brother had died from the police beating. The man marched over to me and touched me on the shoulder with his AK-47. I would have much preferred he touch me with a hand rather than a weapon. Actually, I would have preferred he not touch me at all.

Regardless, I wasn't sure what *his* motives were, but I carried on with mine as he left me to continue his angry parade around the room.

"You guys are not going to win," I said. "Nobody's going to feel sympathy for your death. You die, and they'll fill the bus up and take you to the grave. But that's going to be it."

That was the Holy Spirit giving me that boldness because saying those words in that setting without His prompting would have been stupid.

"But life is precious to God," I continued. "God has a plan for each of you. God loves you."

I stretched out my arms wide, in a non-threatening manner, to depict what Jesus Christ had done for me on the cross. I was near tears at the thought, but the manager sat emotionless. So did all his men, except one whose eyes let slip through a glimpse of compassion that led me to believe the Holy Spirit was working on his heart.

"I have not always been a missionary of the gospel," I said. "I committed many wrongs in my life, but I am an example of God's forgiveness and His transforming power."

I bowed my head and closed my eyes, then began to pray aloud for the men in that basement. As I prayed, I thought about the agitated guy with the gun. I opened one of my eyes to sneak a peek at his demeanor. Not a single head was bowed, not one set of eyes closed. Every one of the drug dealers stared at me as I prayed. I opened my other eye, too, and kept both eyes open through the rest of the prayer.

That wasn't the way I learned to pray growing up in southern Georgia, and in seminary, I hadn't been instructed on how to witness to a roomful of gun-wielding drug dealers. But I've learned in Brazil that sometimes I need to do things differently to communicate the gospel message God has called me to share.

Chapter 1

I Must Make a Difference

The most-asked question of me is why my family and I still are in Brazil.

During our more than twenty years as missionaries here for the Southern Baptist Convention, I've had a weapon pointed into my face nine times, I've had my wife field a death threat against me, I've been hit over the top of the head with a pistol, I've had bullets fly by my head, I've been interrogated by police and accused of drug trafficking, I've had to be tested multiple times for hepatitis and HIV, and I've seen a fellow missionary's dead body dumped into a lake of sewage.

So, it's a good question. I've asked it of myself.

Especially in the seventeen years my family ministered in the slums of Rio de Janeiro. In June 2018, my family moved from Rio to São Paulo when I became the regional strategist for Zone Two.

My work now is more at the 30,000-foot level: setting strategies for planting churches, mentoring seminary students and pastors, and working with leadership back in the States to identify churches there to partner with Brazilian churches. It's a big change from when I was working in Rio de Janeiro's *favelas*—the slums on the edges of the sprawling city of almost seven million people.

The weapons, the death threats, the bullets, and interrogations came in Rio. On our trips back home to the States, the stories of our experiences in Rio elicited exclamations of "Wow!" and questions of, "Are you serious?" If I had not lived out each one, I would also wonder if they were true. Once I assured that my stories were indeed legitimate, the reactions would be along the lines of "You need to write a book" and "This should be a movie."

There have been attempts at a movie, although one has not yet come to fruition. And this book was almost published eight years ago. But after Rio earned the right to host the world-stage events of soccer's World Cup in 2014 and the Summer Olympics in 2016, things started changing in Rio. With the sports world preparing to shine its bright spotlight on Rio not once but twice, Brazil's second-most populous metropolitan area needed to do some cleaning up of the areas controlled by drug cartels or paramilitary groups.

As a pastor, I had been granted special privileges in and around Rio's *favelas* for reasons I'll explain later. Printing a book that revealed who I knew in Rio's hidden hierarchies would have increased the risk for my family and me—and the threat had already been enough without a book. For security reasons, I had to cancel the book.

But now, with those major events behind us and me in a new role in a new city, I sensed the Lord telling me the time had come to share our story of working in the *favelas*. I know that a small number of people are sharing the gospel amid circumstances like I experienced in the *favelas*. But I also know that we are all called to share the gospel, and we all face fears in carrying out what God has called us to do—whether it's in the slums of Rio or the conference room of a downtown high-rise office.

When I share my stories, I don't do so because I want people to tell me, "Pastor Eric, you are such a courageous Christian!" Instead, I share my stories because I want to tell people about my struggles with being courageous. I don't believe the circumstances are all that important. When God calls us to obey Him, it's not contingent on whether the circumstances are favorable.

Honestly, a couple of times in Rio, I decided my assignment was complete, that I was moving my family back to the United States. But I stayed because God called me to be there.

Family members and friends even questioned why I stayed, often adding they were afraid for me. I experienced times when I was fearful for myself, too. I wrestled with fear.

But I have an even greater fear than the one for my life: I am afraid of not doing *with* my life what God has called me to do.

That fear most motivates me.

Peter's sermon in the third chapter of Acts inspires me. It came during the early days of the church. Right before Jesus ascended into heaven, He left His disciples with the Great Commission—a favorite passage of foreign missionaries when they are preaching back in the States because it talks about taking the gospel message into all nations. So, there was Peter, with the gospel beginning to spread to the Gentiles, delivering an impromptu sermon to a group of Jews who had gathered around him after God had used Peter to miraculously heal a lame man.

Peter had a three-point sermon. First, he preached about who Jesus was. Second, Peter called for the sinners among the audience to repent. Then he concluded by issuing a warning to those who reject Jesus, appealing to the Jews' knowledge of the blessing God had promised to the descendants of Abraham.

The final verse of the chapter, verse 26, sticks with me: "To you first, God, having raised up His Servant Jesus, sent Him to bless you, in turning away every one of you from your iniquities" (NKJV).

Peter's message still preaches strong in the twenty-first century. God's desire to bless us includes turning us away from our sins. And that hits home for me because, let me tell you, I have missed the boat too many times, yet I still have been blessed by God in saving me from my sins.

When I think about Acts 3:26, I also cannot help but consider the last part of Matthew 25, where Jesus talks about how when the people had helped feed or clothe "the least of these" in their society, "you did it to Me."

I know what it is like to be poor and needy, and I know what it is like to have needs met. During key moments in my ministry among the poor of Rio, God stepped in and reminded me, "You were hungry, and you were not clothed, and I fed you and clothed you."

Because of the blessings God has given me, my mission in life is to be a vessel through which He can bless others. To do otherwise—to be blessed by God as I have and not be a blessing to others—would be extremely selfish.

There have been times I have wanted to turn my back on my calling. But I can't. I can't say no to God. He has looked upon me and had compassion on me, and I have determined that I will not be a harbor of God's love. I will not allow my life to be one into which God's blessings flow and then become a mere storage place of His love. I *must* share God's love with others.

My life story tells me that I must make a difference.

Living with Little

I grew up part of a poor black family in southern Georgia in the late 1960s and '70s, back when it was still the "Old South." My dad had left home for another woman by the time I was nine years old. Our family was never the same after my father left, and I left home when I was sixteen. I struggled in college, joined the army, and after leaving the army, got into work I should not have been involved in. But all along the way, God was showing me His grace and placing people into my life who would point me to a better life.

While God was working on me, I kept missing the boat. And when I say that, I mean I was *really* missing the boat. Yet God kept giving me grace, and He kept sending boats my way until I finally got on board for where He wanted to take me. Now I can look back and see how every step of the way, God was preparing me for what I do now as a missionary in Brazil.

As the youngest of eight kids in our home, I learned early that if I had anything important to say, I needed to speak up and say it. Otherwise, I probably wouldn't be heard. That was good training for a future missionary, but growing up and even into adulthood, I noticed how the thoughts of a young, poor, black man were not always appreciated. That wasn't only from white folks, but sometimes from other blacks, too. There are plenty of ways other than race that people can deem you to be lesser than them.

My dad was the product of a fling between his mother, who was a maid, and a white man whose home she cleaned. As a result, Dad was a light-skinned black man, and he passed that trait along to me.

Dad was a firm man, a strong man. And loud. When he wanted people to listen to what he had to say, he made sure they heard him. I decided growing up that I wouldn't be loud like my dad. Well, I have that characteristic of his, too.

When there was a dispute among us kids in the house –and with eight of us, there were plenty of those—he stayed out of it at first. But if we didn't resolve the matter on our own, he'd step in. "All right," we'd hear him say with authority from his chair in the living room, "that's enough now. Cut it out." And we did. Dad was strict, and he had long arms that, when we acted up, seemed like they could reach all the way across the living room. I joke that we could do something that would get us in trouble and get a minute-long head start running from Dad, and he could still reach out and grab us before we got away.

The angrier Dad became, the louder his voice grew. So, we didn't push things too far when Dad was around because when he got angry, he would be quick to lash out, and we feared Dad's anger.

But Dad had another side to him, too. From the same chair in which he would yell at us, he could also sit completely quiet as he read his newspaper. And at church, where he was a deacon, he was such a smiling, happy, outgoing guy that members of our church would have been stunned to see the angry side we witnessed at home.

They would not have suspected him as someone who would leave our mother for a younger woman who lived down our street. But that's what he did.

I don't think I had come to know Dad well before he left. For some reason, we seemed to have an arms-length relationship.

I was, however, very close to my Momma. I don't know how she managed to raise eight kids as a single mother. God must have provided her with a special, extra helping of grace. She took us to Union Missionary Baptist Church almost every week, and she also allowed me to go with friends to their churches. Visiting friends' churches exposed me to Southern Baptist churches, Pentecostal Holiness churches, and seemingly every type of church in between. Momma didn't care how many different churches I went to because she wanted to make sure that her kids grew up establishing a foundation in church.

Momma rented a small, wooden house off a country dirt road in the community of Putney, a few miles south of Albany, Georgia. Our house had a tin roof, and when it rained hard, it got so loud inside that we had to yell to be heard above the sound of the rain pelting the roof. Within walking distance, north of where we lived, was a black neighborhood with what we thought were really nice houses. The homes weren't nice in our neighborhood, with the exception of Mr. Davis's. He was an insurance salesman, and he owned a brick home that to us meant he was wealthy.

We had chicken pens for eggs to eat and pig pens to raise pigs we could sell to be butchered. My brother Clifford and I helped out our family's finances by picking pecans. When I was elementary school-aged, we worked Saturdays at a drag strip about half a mile from our house. We walked to the drag strip and worked from 9:30 in the morning until three or four o'clock in the afternoon, picking up cans and trash for five dollars per day plus lunch. Five bucks was a lot of money to us back then, and it was a big deal when we didn't get paid our five bucks for the last day we worked there.

There also was an automobile auction business next to the highway through Putney. We would wander by that place, listen to the auctioneer quickly move an automobile to the next buyer, and pick out which cars we wanted as we fantasized about one day having enough money to own a car.

I had a friend in the nicer neighborhood north of us, and I would walk up the highway to his house. He had a BB gun, and as a kid who didn't have much, I thought his owning a BB gun was one of the coolest things ever. One day we were shooting his gun, and I accidentally hit a window on one of his neighbors' houses. The glass shattered. We didn't try to hide what had happened and admitted our transgression, but my friend's mother still was none too pleased. She paid to replace the neighbor's window but told my friend, "I don't want that kid over here no more," and forbid him from having me over to play. Her words made me feel like she was looking down on me because her family had more money than mine.

Although we were poor, I didn't have a poor kid's mindset. One big reason was because of my Shetland pony. That little horse made me feel like a big man.

I received the Shetland as a surprise gift when I was six or seven. Momma purchased it for twenty-five dollars on a payment plan that allowed her a full year to pay it off.

I rode my Shetland everywhere I could. I couldn't afford a saddle, so I laid a burlap sack across the horse's back when I rode him. It was on that pony that I discovered that horses don't like snakes. I was riding down our dirt road when my horse saw a snake. He stopped dead in his tracks, and I kept going—right over the top of his head and nose-first into the road.

I even wanted to ride my Shetland to school one day when I missed the bus, but Momma wouldn't let me. I had no plan for where I would have kept the horse at school or how I would have fed him during the day, but I didn't want to miss school. Back then, if we missed the bus, we missed all our classes because we didn't have anyone who could drive us to school.

Growing up in Putney was a good time for me. We were close to the people around us, and it was safe for us to roam our neighborhood and play. We lived in the poorest part of town, but we were among good people. It seemed like everyone in the neighborhood looked for ways to take care of each other, even down to something as small as the first person to the mailboxes, grabbing mail from all the boxes and delivering the mail to each person's house on the way back to his home.

My Momma's attitude kept me from growing up resentful of white people, but I did observe negative black-white attitudes around me.

There was a white man who drove his truck down our road and sold produce, including watermelons and tomatoes. He honked his horn as he drove slowly through our neighborhood and yelled through the window what he had for sale. Just a piece down the road lived a family whose kids were real hell-raisers. They always seemed to be pulling off mischievous stunts, and one day when I was still really young, the white man stopped his truck near their house and began selling his produce.

When the man wasn't watching, those kids grabbed one of the watermelons off his truck and placed it in front of one of the truck's tires. When the man climbed back into the driver's seat, I yelled out, "Hey, there's a watermelon that fell off the truck!"

"Shut yo mouth!" the pranksters scolded me.

The driver didn't hear me and waved as he started to drive away. The kids smiled and waved back as the watermelon exploded in every direction under the truck's weight. Those kids were proud of themselves for busting up one of the white man's watermelons as if that had taught him some kind of important life lesson.

Our neighborhood contained an eerie reminder of the racial tensions of southern Georgia. A large tree close to our house had been used for hanging slaves. A white man owned the land, and there were people who argued that he should cut down the tree. Because he wouldn't cut it down, some of us thought he might have been a member of the Ku Klux Klan, although nothing to the like was ever proven. But, still, that tree was an ugly reminder of a time that had produced too many attitudes that remained prevalent in our community.

Perhaps the biggest benefit of living where we did come in education. The kids in our neighborhood were bussed to Radium Springs Elementary School in an all-white neighborhood. Momma didn't receive a good education growing up, and she wanted one for us more than anything else. Momma had only a seventh-grade education, but by being bussed to what had been an all-white school, we had nothing but the best of the best in our school.

The classrooms were nice, and the teachers were good. I got my first girlfriend at Radium Springs Elementary—sort of, because Ms. Reed, my math teacher, never knew she was my girlfriend.

Ms. Reed had to be six feet tall and had long hair that flowed down her back. I wanted to marry her. I told one of my friends, "That is the most beautiful black woman I've ever met in my life. She has got to be the one for me. I'm going to buy her a pencil!"

So, I bought her a one-cent pencil and presented it to her. She smiled as she accepted my gift, and when I looked at that smile, I was in love. For Valentine's Day, I gave her a valentine with a big, red heart and the words, "Will you be mine?" I did not have great grades in every class, but I sure did well in Ms. Reed's math class!

Father Figure

When my dad ran off with the younger woman, things began to spiral out of control in our house. Dad's departure revealed how much structure he had brought to our household, and without the order, he brought to our home, our family suffered. I had some brothers and sisters who went crazy with acting up, and I'm sure their anger toward Dad contributed to their actions.

I think I was the only one of us kids who didn't grow up angry with Dad for what he did, perhaps because I was the youngest. Despite what Dad did to Momma, I never heard her say anything bad about him.

We had been poor with our dad. Without him, we were dirt poor.

Momma started cleaning houses to make money. She had a great work ethic and took pride in her work. She cleaned up after others and never complained, washing, and scrubbing as though she were cleaning Jesus' own house. Momma got her hands and knees dirty because she loved her kids and wanted to provide for us.

One of the people whose homes Momma cleaned liked her work so much that he recommended her for a job pressing clothes in a dry-cleaning store. Even with that job, it didn't take long for Momma to go through her money with rent to pay and all our mouths to feed.

We ate a lot of ketchup sandwiches growing up. If you've never had one, the recipe is simple: take two slices of bread, squirt ketchup on one of them, close the sandwich, and chow down. Some days, ketchup and bread were all we had in the house to eat. I'm embarrassed to admit this now because it was the wrong thing to do even considering our circumstances, but there were plentiful cornfields near us, and when we got hungry while the corn was in season, my siblings and I would go steal enough ears of corn for everyone in the house to eat.

I remember one day when there was nothing to eat in our house. Our cupboards were as bare as Old Mother Hubbard's, and Momma didn't have the money to buy any groceries. We were all hungry, and everybody in the house was quiet most of the day.

Around five o'clock, a man from our church we called Deacon Colbert knocked on the door and handed over three bags full of groceries. He said he had been at work, and the Lord had impressed upon him that he needed to bless our family. Deacon Colbert definitely blessed us because we did not know where our next meal was coming from. So, when I worked in the slums of Rio and God reminded me that he had fed me when I was hungry, I knew precisely why it was important that I follow God's calling to be a blessing to others.

I had occasional contact with my dad after he left. However, because I hadn't been that close to him, what I missed more than my dad was just having *a* dad around the house. The two things most lacking for me in my father's absence were structure in our family and having a man to talk to.

Despite her best efforts, Momma was unable to fill the void my dad left in our home. A boy needs his father, and there's no way to get around that. But at Radium Springs Middle School, I met someone who became like a father to me. My football and cross-country coach, Bobby McGhee, was the man who gave me a vision for my life.

Coach McGhee was a black man coaching and teaching in a mostly white school. I became close friends with his son Vincent, and that provided me the opportunity to visit the McGhee home often and see Coach outside of the school setting. The entire McGhee family took me in and loved on me.

They lived in a nice, middle-class neighborhood. It was a lengthy walk to their home, but back then, walking long distances wasn't a big deal. *The Cosby Show* wasn't on television yet, but in some regards being in the McGhees' home felt like visiting the Huxtables' home.

Except, Coach, although talkative at school, was much quieter at home than the Huxtable father. Coach didn't say much unless you did something that needed to be corrected. But just the presence he maintained in his home was enough of an example for me. He provided for his home what my family had been missing since my dad had left. Being in Coach's home allowed me to observe how a properly functioning family operated.

I was cutting up in homeroom one day when Coach jumped my case in front of the class. He got my attention and stared into my eyes. "Buddy," he said, using the name he called just about everyone, "let me tell you something. One day you are going to be the breadwinner of your own family, and you're going to need something up there in your head that helps you provide food for your family. So, stop being a class clown and get some intelligence in you. Do you understand? Stop doing this."

When he said that, for some reason, it hit me that one day I would be the provider for a family. Perhaps I had not thought of that before because there wasn't a man in our family who was the breadwinner. But whatever the reason, that short remark from Coach McGhee signaled to me that he believed in me. Even though I had no clue what

Coach saw in me, I had never had an adult male express his belief that I could become somebody.

I was eating with the McGhees on Thanksgiving shortly after the homeroom incident, and when we were where the rest of his family couldn't hear us, Coach told me, "Let me tell you something, Buddy. The only reason I called you down in class the other day is that I'm seeing you get with the wrong group of people. You will only go as far as the people you put yourself around."

Coach McGhee was correct; I had not been choosing my friends wisely. I was hanging around guys who were fighters. They talked about violence a lot, and how they were going to beat up this guy and that guy, and they boasted about how many girlfriends they had. After Thanksgiving, I dropped those friends like hot potatoes and started making new friends who were courteous to the teachers and made good grades.

My new friends' conversations were completely different. They talked about which universities they wanted to attend, and I'd never heard anything like that from the other group. They talked about girls, too, but in a respectful manner. Partly because of their positive influence, I focused more on studying. My old friends didn't like me leaving them and would say things like, "He's trying to be white." But what they said didn't bother me. In fact, it only affirmed about them what Coach had said. And now, as I keep up with the new set of friends I had made, I see that every one of them has become successful businessmen.

Coach also once told me, "The sign of an intelligent man is the ability to adjust to any given situation. You are intelligent, and you've got to have the ability to adjust. When you're out in the streets, you've got to be able to adjust, to be able to talk to anyone. People will judge you based on your grammar and the way you speak. So, I encourage you: you need to use your English correctly."

I had already taken note of Coach's grammar and how well he spoke. In my neighborhood, we used a lot of slang. One day I walked into the McGhees' house and said, "Yo, yo, yo." Coach immediately shot back, "No, no, no."

"Son," he sternly advised, "we don't say, 'Yo, yo, yo.' We say, 'May I speak to you?' Or 'May I have your attention?'"

Coach wasn't my English teacher, but because of his influence, I began to clean up my grammar and tried to speak clearly.

Coach McGhee wouldn't have claimed he was like a father to me, but he knew he was. Coach opened the window to a different world for me—one in which a black man could lead a family, live in a beautiful home, and make enough money to drive nice cars.

And he believed *I* had the ability to do that.

Chapter 2

Sensing a Call

While I was in middle school, my Momma set a great example of how to handle racism. We were in a store parking lot when Momma bumped another car with hers. Bumped might be too strong of a word. The cars barely came together, but the young white man driving the other car jumped out and yelled at my Momma, calling her a "stupid n-word."

I didn't understand why the man was reacting so angrily, but I became even more confused when I noticed a cross on the man's shirt.

Momma was calm when she got back into the car, but the look on her face revealed the man's words had shaken her. While she seemed at ease on the outside, I was mad inside and out. I didn't like the man treating my Momma that way and had no problem with her seeing my anger.

"Didn't that hurt your feelings?" I asked her.

"No," she said in a soft tone.

By watching Momma, who had more of a right than the other driver to be angry because of what he had called her, I learned a valuable lesson about meekness. Meekness is power under control. Too many people confuse meekness with weakness. In Numbers 12:3, the New King James Version describes Moses as "very meek" but "above all the men which were upon the face of the earth."

Moses wasn't weak; he had power under control. My Momma wasn't weak either, and she demonstrated that in the parking lot.

What I took from that incident is that no matter how right I might be, there are occasions when it is the wrong time to say something, and it's better to remain quiet. During my years as a missionary in Brazil, I've had to go back to that lesson and keep my mouth shut.

Finding Common Ground

At Radium Springs Middle School, some momentum began to build among my black friends that I could win the school's all-sports trophy. The award took into account all-around athletic accomplishments and grades. It wasn't that I was a great athlete—I was good-sized and a good football player, but not a great all-around athlete—or that I made great grades. But my friends figured I was the black student with the best chance of winning.

"Reese, you go win it," my black friends encouraged me. "We'll even help you with your grades."

They never helped me with any of my classwork!

I set my sights on winning the award. I was the type of person who believed I could do anything until I tried and failed. And even then, I still wouldn't be so sure I wouldn't succeed if I tried again.

One day in Coach McGhee's class, I was feeling confident—more accurately, overconfident—in my athletic abilities and told Joey, a white kid who could run like a deer, that I could beat him in a four-lap race on the school's track.

Joey said he could beat me, and when neither of us backed down from our stances, Coach halted class and took us all out to the track for a race between Joey and me.

When the race started, Joey took off faster than a deer. I knew I wasn't as fast as Joey, but as a runner on the cross-country team, I believed I could outlast him. So, I let him take off at his fast pace and convinced myself that Joey would tire because of the distance, and I'd catch him on the fourth lap.

We never made it to the final lap.

On the third lap, Joey was so far out ahead of me that Coach McGhee halted the race early and sent everyone back to the classroom.

I guess I should have been embarrassed at being trounced in front of the entire class, but that wasn't my style. "He got me this time," I told my friends as if I would beat Joey the next time we raced. But we didn't race again, and I didn't wind up winning the all-sports trophy.

Our family moved from Putney to the south side of Albany before I completed middle school. The government handed out vouchers enabling families to move out of projects and low-income areas, and my Momma received one. Our new home was on a paved road instead of a dirt one. My brother Clifford and I were able to have a room to ourselves instead of having to share one with two of our sisters, and no longer living under a tin roof, we all were able to sleep on rainy nights.

The move meant a change in schools, and that meant leaving Coach McGhee. But his influence stayed with me.

Instead of being bussed to a predominantly white school as before, I now was attending an all-black school close enough to home that I could ride a bicycle to and from activities at school instead of having to find someone to give me a ride. Southside Junior High's environment was completely different from the one at Radium Springs.

I was offered a marijuana joint for the first time at my new school. At first, I thought it was a joke. But when I realized the offer was serious, I turned it down for two reasons. First, an older brother had used marijuana and, later, crack cocaine, and I remembered seeing how much that broke Momma's heart. I couldn't break Momma's heart like that. Second, I thought back to my visits to the McGhees's home and my desire to have their family structure when I became an adult. I knew drugs destroyed families, so I wasn't going to have anything to do with drugs and risk derailing my goal.

Graduating junior high meant another cross-town school assignment to Westover High School.

I had been in a predominantly white middle school and then an all-black junior high and being a part of two schools with extreme racial makeups prepared me well for the mixed-race student body of Westover. I was able to find common ground between the blacks and the whites at Westover and intentionally worked to not take a position on either side of black-white debates.

Instead, I tried to get each side to consider the other side's point of view. I would hear a black friend say something like "That white guy …," and I would come back at him with a question like, "Have you ever considered thinking about it this way?" Or when a black friend would say, "I don't trust white people as far as I can throw them," I would respond, "What are you throwing white people for? You shouldn't be throwing white people at all. "Because of my middle school and junior high experiences, I knew how those on both sides of an issue were thinking.

It also helped me immensely that I became good friends there with Victor Tolbert and Ellery Farrell. Victor and Ellery were both black, and a grade above me, and they were like the positive-influence friends I had made in junior high because they kept an open mind about things. We hung out together and had some thought-provoking conversations. As with my friends in junior high, Victor and Ellery also were successful after graduating from Westover.

I made the Westover Patriots football team and played outside linebacker. Playing on the team allowed me to see for the first time what good could result when blacks and white worked together toward a common goal. That was when I learned that if you give people a reason to look beyond skin color and dollar amounts in bank accounts, they can see something different. I remembered that later as I got into the ministry and realized that what I want people to see more than anything else is Jesus.

Preacher or Lawyer?

When I was sixteen, I moved out of my Momma's home. I didn't like what had become of our home after my dad left, and at sixteen, when I had the first opportunity to leave, I did. I worked at a McDonald's, and a lady rented me a mobile home for one hundred dollars per month. I had no furniture in my trailer and slept on a mattress on the floor.

I hate to say it was a relief to be out living on my own at that young age, but it was. I couldn't put up any longer with what was going on at home.

Thankfully, my Momma had helped me establish a spiritual foundation in the church. In addition to going to church with Momma on Sundays and visiting friends' churches when I was a kid, a white church across town had brought a bus through our neighborhood and other poor neighborhoods that took us to church, where we were given candy and the gospel message. I ate up both. During one of those Saturday outreaches, I accepted Jesus as my Savior. I was six, but I knew I needed Jesus, and I understood what my decision meant.

At the time I moved out on my own, my spiritual awareness as a

Christian remained strong. There were a couple of local preachers who allowed me to travel with them when they preached revivals out of town and hearing them preaching and talking with them during the car rides opened my mind to the possibility of becoming a minister. One day as I was driving to school in either my junior or senior year, I sensed God calling me to preach.

I was like, *God, you don't want me to preach. Can you check my Social Security number and see if you've got the right dude?*

I must have been the right dude because that sense of calling didn't go away. I don't know why, but I didn't tell anyone at first. Later, I told a few friends I was thinking about becoming a preacher.

Now, I was a talker in high school. I could debate and argue with the best of them. My friends had an idea for my career choice that they thought was better than becoming a minister.

"You need to be a lawyer, not a preacher," they would tell me. "You can debate. You're an intelligent man."

But I kept telling them that something inside me was telling me I needed to become a preacher. One of those times, a friend came back with a question that grabbed my attention.

"Eric," he asked me flat out, "do you realize that black preachers live on very meager salaries and die poor?"

I didn't fact-check my friend's claim. But I had been poor all my life. Living in a trailer with no furniture, I was still poor. I didn't want to remain poor, and my friend's question influenced me to resist my calling.

Into the Army

After graduating from Westover in 1984, I enrolled at Albany State College (now Albany State University), a historically black college in my hometown. Because I had been a good football player in high school, I planned to try out for the football team as a walk-on and play without a scholarship in hopes of landing a scholarship for future seasons.

But I developed interests other than football and didn't focus on the sport. I had let myself get out of shape, too, and I didn't make the team. When I began my freshman year, I became more successful socially and found that more appealing than sports.

I achieved a level of popularity early on, and my friends encouraged me to run for freshman class president. I intended to until I learned of another candidate named Kim. She was pretty and nice, so I approached her with an idea: I told her I had friends encouraging me to run for president, too, but I would be willing to run alongside her as her vice-presidential candidate. We ran together on the ticket, brought our supporters together, and won the election. Thus, I became part of the school's political leadership.

I joined the college debate team and had success there. Some thought with my ability to debate, I had the makings of a lawyer. But one member of the team disagreed. "You don't need to try to be a lawyer," she told me. "You need to be a preacher."

What are you talking about? I thought. *I'm no preacher.*

Being on the debate team placed me in a position where my voice could be heard. Still inspired by Coach McGhee, I wanted to have an even wider influence than through the debate team.

One of my goals had been to change society by helping people learn to discuss—and hopefully resolve—issues peacefully. I created an on-campus club called Black Men in Unity. Our aim was to help young black men strive for significance in their lives by breaking out of the limited possibilities for success we had been conditioned to believe existed because of our skin color.

We hosted open debates that covered racial issues, and for one event, we invited a group to our campus that held the opposite view of our students' belief that the Confederate Battle Emblem should be removed from the Georgia state flag. About 80 students attended, and at the beginning of the meeting, I walked up on the platform and said, "Listen, no matter what our guests say, we need to be responsible in what we say and how we respond to what's said. We need to know that higher education is a learning field where we can choose the types of decisions we make. We want to take all the emotions out of this, and we want to keep it strictly academic." Everyone in the auditorium clapped—our students and our guests.

Our club emphasized responsibility and being productive in society. We held outreaches that targeted teenaged black boys in Albany as recipients of our message. It was my way of trying to say, "Please stop black-on-black crime. Stop not going to school. And pull your pants up." Now it's known as sagging, and it was one of my biggest pet peeves whenever we were around the young boys. I ranted and ranted about, "Pull your pants up, man. Get your pants up. What part of corporate America is going to let you walk around with your pants down?"

The group members knew what was coming every time, and they would whisper to the teenagers, "Pull your pants up before we get started because he's going to call you out. So just go ahead and do it now."

My participation in various activities resulted in me receiving a bit of attention on campus. That attention certainly was not something I was seeking. Because I was often out-front speaking and leading, some students suggested I had a future in politics. But one student told me, "You don't need to be a politician. You need to be a preacher."

Combined with the earlier comment from the debate team member, I wondered if this was a second word, or a second calling, from God for my life. If it was, I didn't heed it. I believed that my best potential for making a long-lasting impact was through my efforts toward making social changes, especially among young black men. I considered the absence of male leaders in the black community a fundamental problem.

But while I was busy with all my activities and trying to be popular, my grades suffered, and I wound up on academic probation. I think my poor grades landed me on popularity probation, too.

That sent me back to Pam, a girl I had dated in high school but had moved on from once I started meeting other females at Albany State. After Pam and I started dating again, she joined the army and tried to convince me to do the same. She had this thought-out plan by which I would also enlist, we would marry, and then the army would station us together.

Being on academic probation, not making the football team, watching my popularity wane, and scraping by financially, I felt like a failure. I signed up for Pam's plan and enlisted in the army.

After basic training, where I was made a platoon leader largely because I had attended college, I was stationed at Fort Lee in Virginia and later transferred to Fort Bragg in North Carolina. While I was in North Carolina, Pam was at Fort Drum in New York. Our long-distance relationship was working until I started getting busy with working my way up at Fort Bragg. With my competitive nature, I put more time into the competition for advancement through the ranks than I did our relationship. The clincher for Pam came when I neglected to mail her a birthday card.

The next time I called Pam, she pointed out that I had missed her birthday. "I don't think I'm in love with you," she told me. "I think another guy here likes me."

I didn't take getting dumped too well. I started punching the metal beds and lockers in our barracks, and some of the guys called for the chaplain, who asked why I wanted to kill myself.

"I don't want to kill myself, man," I told him, surprised at his question. "It's just a girl thing. I'm okay."

I rented a car and drove to see Pam in New York. But Pam was done with me. Our relationship was over. She had been the main reason I had joined the army, but after we broke up, I could put full concentration into my service duties.

At the time, I was a supply specialist in an aviation unit and a squad leader. I began driving for a colonel who one day told me, "Private, you have some good leadership skills. Have you ever thought about going back to college and getting a degree?"

I took the colonel's question to heart and began thinking about taking another shot at college.

Prejudice at Church

At the same time, I was getting my spiritual life back in shape. After keeping God on the back burner for a couple of years, I began to make room for Him in my life again. I attended an all-white, Independent Fundamental Baptist church. Even though I was a light-skinned black man and conservative, I was warmly accepted.

That church taught me how to share my faith. I disagreed with certain beliefs the church held, but let me tell you, that church did believe in witnessing. I have been a part of churches that talked about sharing their faith, but it was more like "Come and see us." Those folks in that church knew how to go out and get 'em. My evangelism training with them was second to none.

My high point at the church came when I was asked to preach a five-minute "sermon" during a New Year's Eve service. It was my first sermon. Those who know me now would be surprised to learn I could preach a sermon in only five minutes.

The low point in that church came when I was having what should have been considered success during the church's visitation campaign. One Sunday, a big-named speaker was scheduled to speak, and there was a big push to pack the church. I went out and visited blacks and Hispanics and invited them for that Sunday. When six of them showed up, the white members looked awkwardly at them and didn't speak to them. One of the black men I invited came up to me with an angry look on his face and sarcastically remarked, "Thanks, brother, for bringing me to church with you."

One of the members told me, "Brother Eric, there is a black preacher down the road who is a great friend of this church, and your friends can go to his church."

Instead of the visitors' skin color, the church members should have focused on the fact that they weren't saved. The state of their souls was what should have been the most important thing.

I didn't understand the church's cold shoulder toward the blacks and Hispanics. Partly because I didn't understand, I decided not to leave the church right away so I could try to gain insight into the members' thinking. But I knew not to invite any more minorities—more for the minorities' sake than the church members' sake as far as I was concerned.

Also, there was a young white lady in the church who seemed attracted to me. That didn't go over well, either. Some members claimed God didn't like for races to mix, citing as biblical proof the story of Samson and the problems caused by his attraction to Philistine women. Of course, a study of Samson's story reveals their misapplication of Scripture.

It wasn't too much later, in 1989, that I completed my time in the army and returned home to re-enroll at Albany State. Upon returning to Albany, I visited a white Southern Baptist church in town, and when I walked up to the door, a gentleman met me and asked, "What do you need, sir?"

"I'm coming to church," I said.

"No," he told me, "we don't mix here. There's a church down the road that you can attend."

With that and my experience at the North Carolina church, I decided I was tired of Christianity. I had a friend who had kept trying to convince me that, as he would put it, "Christianity is a white man's religion." He had also told me many times, "You just can't trust white people, man. Every time, they're going to choose their own people over you."

For the first time, I started to award credibility to his beliefs. But each time when I would consider that perhaps he was right, after all, the Holy Spirit would speak to my heart, *That's not good counsel.*

Finally, I had to tell my close friend, "That's not right. I just won't believe it."

Although I wouldn't agree with my friend that Christianity was a white man's religion, I was beginning to decide that it wasn't for me.

Chapter 3

Into the Ministry

Back home, I fell back into making bad decisions. I made poor choices in whom I dated. I began drinking alcohol. I lived merely an unanticipated flip of my anger switch from getting into a fight. It was as though I was back to living in the poor community with its fight-to-survive mentality. Ready to fight anyone in a minute, I picked up the nickname "Mike Tyson." I was filled with anger and rage.

I went back to work at McDonald's for the same manager as before. He made me a shift manager because of the time I had spent in the military and the leadership skills I had picked up.

I was bringing home about $150 a week. Wanting to impress my girlfriend, I bought a brand-new Volkswagen. I couldn't afford it, and it got repossessed.

A friend of a friend, who always seemed loaded with cash, asked if I wanted to work in his "operation." When he took me out to eat at a Japanese restaurant and left a $100 tip for the waiter, I recognized an easy way to relieve my financial pressures. I knew I shouldn't have gotten involved, but I didn't have the faith to trust God for other means of financial support.

I told my manager at McDonald's I was quitting my job.

"How can you do this, man?" he asked. "You are the only black manager we have here. I went to bat for you, man. You came back, and we put you right into management."

I couldn't blame him for being upset, but I also could not tell him why I was leaving.

Not surprisingly, I didn't know how to manage my money. I owned four cars parked on campus at one point. The money was so good that even though I knew within a matter of days of starting my new job that I had made a mistake, I stayed with it.

But when some bad things happened within the operation, I told the boss I wanted out. To encourage me not to quit, he had some of his guys put a whuppin' on me. They beat me to a pulp and left me on the side of a road. A passing motorist saw me, stopped, and took me to the hospital. I spent two days in the hospital with a concussion, a fractured rib, and a whole lot of bruises.

I couldn't stay in Albany. Upon my release from the hospital, I fled to Atlanta to hide in the big city, not even sticking around long enough to withdraw from school. A friend took care of that for me. If I had shown my face around Albany one more time, I might have wound up in a mortuary instead of a hospital.

I spent seven months in Atlanta, living in my Toyota Corolla the whole time. I got a part-time job cleaning up at a gas station. I was paid only in gas and food.

Living in my car, I spent a lot of time studying my Bible and crying out to God, asking Him to forgive and restore me. I recommitted my life to God and sensed Him telling me to return to Albany.

On my way back into my hometown, I got pulled over for having a taillight out. That's when I learned there was a warrant out for my arrest. Right before high-tailing it to Atlanta, I had written a check for $573 to purchase alcohol for the members of our club. But when I had said I wanted out of the operation, someone pulled money out of the club's account, so the check bounced, leaving me on the hook for writing a hot check. When I went to bond out, though, no record could be found in the computer system for my name. I still can't explain how that happened other than to say that God granted me a reprieve.

I was still afraid for my life when I returned to live in my trailer, so I kept a weapon on me and kept my eyes open. A former football teammate worked in law enforcement, and when I told him of my situation, he told me he would arrange to have the police keep an eye on my trailer.

Returning to live in Albany created the opportunity to spend time with my dad. Although he had left our family when I was nine, I wouldn't say he had left my life. I always loved my dad and thought of him often. While my brothers and sisters blamed him, I remained grateful to him because he had helped bring me into this world. If that were all he had ever done for me, that would have been enough for me to love and honor him.

I had learned while in the army that my dad was experiencing difficulties with epilepsy, and I sent parts of my military checks to him to help pay for the medications he needed. After moving back to Albany, I stopped by his place from time to time to check on him. It wasn't a regular routine—more of when I was near his home and had time to stop. My visits were short, rarely more than ten minutes, and they were more to make sure he was doing okay and had what he needed. But the more times I stopped, the more we began to connect.

I wanted to have Dad more involved in my life. I was twenty-three and a young man who had already lived out on his own and served in the military. But even an independent young man needs his dad's presence in his life.

One day, Dad tearfully asked my forgiveness for what he had done to Momma and our family. Of course, I accepted. I learned a lesson in humility from my dad—a grown man asking his youngest son for forgiveness. I knew it had to be difficult to admit his mistakes and ask my forgiveness. You can never be too big to say you're sorry, and it's never too late to ask for forgiveness.

My dad and I began going out to eat hot dogs together or just to drive around town. Being in the car was our excuse to get away by ourselves and talk.

I have wonderful memories of the times we sat on his front porch. One of those times we were chatting when out of nowhere, Dad said, "I know I've done some bad things. But you must know that I have always loved you." That was the first time I could remember him saying he loved me. But just as he was saying the final "you," he started going into a shaking rage. He was having a seizure. I'd never seen him have a seizure. I started hollering, "Hey! Hey! Somebody get out here!"

My stepmom came running out of the house, held Dad as still as she could, and put some of his medicine into his mouth. He calmed enough to take one of his pills.

From that point on, Dad started looking for ways to show me that he loved me. He had a beard, and he'd reach over and try to kiss me on the cheek. I cherished his beard, scratching against my shaved face.

One time he told me, "You made me proud, and you're going to make it and go a long way." He'd never told me he was proud of me, and every kid wants to know their parents are proud of them. I always gravitated toward people who believed in me, like Coach McGhee, and when my dad affirmed me and told me I was going to do good things in life, it felt like he was placing a type of ritual blessing upon my head.

That moment came at an important time because I was starting to make key changes in my lifestyle. I'd decided I would have to be an idiot to turn back to my reckless way of living, and I stayed true to the recommitment I'd made to Christ while living in my car in Atlanta.

I re-enrolled at Albany State and immediately joined a Bible study led by Bennett Caldwell, a campus advisor with Religious Life Organization. Mrs. Caldwell had led a Bible study I had attended my first go-round at the school.

A Church to Call Home

Albany is the home of Sherwood Baptist Church, a church now widely known for producing the movies *Flywheel*, *Facing the Giants*, *Fireproof*, and *Courageous*. All I knew about the church at the time was that it was Southern Baptist, traditional, and white.

I was flipping television channels one day when I came across a church service from Sherwood. The pastor, Michael Catt, was preaching, and although he wasn't preaching a hellfire-and-brimstone message, I liked how he was direct in what he was saying. I had heard in the past that Southern Baptists were liberals and racists, and I had wondered how a liberal could be racist. Because I picked up a good first impression from the pastor, I decided to visit Sherwood and investigate whether a liberal could indeed be racist. I liked the church enough to want to keep visiting. Each time I would show up after service had started, took a seat on the back pew, kept my "Amens" to myself, and left right before the service ended. I knew as a black man that I wouldn't be able to hide, but because of my experiences with the church in North Carolina, I didn't want to draw any extra attention to myself. This was southern Georgia in the early '90s; I was pleased enough that I had been able to make it inside a Southern Baptist church. So, I slipped in and slipped out without getting to know anyone, although I was always greeted with friendly smiles from the people I made eye contact with.

That routine went on for a month until one Sunday morning, Pastor Catt ended his sermon a little early, asked an associate pastor to close the service, left the pulpit, walked up the aisle, and came right up to me. He introduced himself, shook my hand, and said, "Glad to have you here. Welcome." Then he gave me a big hug!

From that point, I was sold on the church. (And still am. Sherwood Baptist is our home church when we are in the States.) The following Sunday, I made it to church early enough to attend Sunday school. It wasn't long until I joined the church and became an official member.

I had noticed one other black man at services. After I got to know some people, I was surprised to learn the man earlier had been elected as the church's first black deacon. Other deacons had left the church as a result, but Pastor Catt said, "As far I'm concerned, the man is qualified. He has led twenty-four members of the church to Christ."

Pastor Catt's welcoming of me wasn't a one-time occurrence. He remained intentional about greeting me at services and invited me to his office so we could talk more and get to know each other. He also invited me into his family's home for a meal. He had two young daughters then, and trust me, at that time in that part of Georgia, there weren't many white dads inviting a single, young black man into his home. I assumed the man didn't know the rules.

I had a roommate run up a big light bill and move out. I didn't have enough money to pay the bill, and when Pastor Catt found out, he arranged to have my bill paid.

It wasn't only Pastor Catt, though, who made me want to remain at Sherwood Baptist. He was the one who took the first steps to welcome me personally, but I would not have stayed if the members of his church hadn't backed up his words with their actions. The people made me feel like I belonged in the church, and I, in turn, was sold out to Sherwood. I was so serious about "my" church that I started taking my tithes to the church office during the middle of the week when I got paid instead of waiting until the Sunday offering. My tithe was only about twenty bucks, but it was my tithe, and I was determined to give it as soon as I could. I was bringing it to 'em, man. As a missionary and former pastor, let me tell you, when someone's paying tithes in the middle of the week, they are completely on board.

The pastor's wife, Terri, taught the singles Sunday school class, and she wanted me to get involved with a church outreach for Albany State because of my knowledge of the school. I told Terri that I had noticed students there during the winter months who weren't wearing coats, and she was all over that opportunity. The church started a coat collection, and we went onto campus and handed out coats. Let's just say that my stock rose on campus. I was walking around with a white woman handing out free coats. "What's going on, Reese?" the students would ask me. "You done made it, man!"

I hadn't made it, and although their reason was off, I would say that I was beginning to make it. I owed a huge debt of gratitude to the Catts and members of Sherwood Baptist for accepting me. They didn't care about my skin color. They saw me as a brother—their brother in Christ.

Dad's Legacy

While all this spiritual growth was occurring for me, I lost my dad. He was sitting on the front porch one day, chewing tobacco, when he had a seizure and choked to death on the tobacco.

As much as Dad's passing hurt, I was so grateful that over the previous year and a half, we had been able to partially make up for the lost years. Our relationship at the end of his life was great, and I was thankful to have that.

I preached at Dad's funeral, drawing from his life story to talk about how there is never a time when you can't make a wrong a right. I shared how my dad taught me what it was like to be a real man. I disclosed that my dad had hurt me greatly through his actions and then added that we all were capable of hurting others as my dad had hurt me.

"You may have hurt someone," I said, "but if God can teach you a lesson that came from my dad, it's that it's never too late while you're still breathing on this side of the dirt to go to that person and say, 'I wronged you. Please forgive me.'"

I read from Matthew 5, the Sermon on the Mount, where Jesus instructed us to "let your 'Yes' by 'Yes,' and your 'No,' 'No.'" (NKJV)

"Just in case you've had a 'Yes' that you didn't fulfill, go back, and make it right," I said. Then I repeated for emphasis, "Go back and make it right."

During the service, I looked down from the platform to my brothers and sisters seated at the front of the church. I knew even after Dad's death that some of them remained angry with him. Here I was, the youngest of us siblings, preaching, and I looked at them and called each of them by name.

"What I've learned in life," I told them, "is that you don't always get it right and that you make mistakes. But the big person says, 'I made a mistake. Please forgive me.' I know if Daddy was alive now, he'd be asking that you forgive him. Some of us got a chance. Some didn't."

Then I said to the rest of the church, "You might have wronged someone, or you might have been wronged by someone. The big person asks for forgiveness and tries to reconcile relationships. That's what I encourage you to do. Let your 'Yes' be 'Yes,' and your 'No' be 'No.' Try to reconcile your differences."

Because of the message that I was able to share with those at the funeral, I'd say that despite the mistakes he made, my dad left behind a good legacy.

Meeting My Greatest Treasure

I still carried the inspiration from my dad's telling me he was proud of me. His words of encouragement had kick-started my competitive nature. Knowing that my dad loved me and was proud of me, my attitude became, *It's on now! I'm going to go somewhere!*

I was serious about school and progressing toward a degree. I was taking part in a good Bible study on campus. I had found a great church in Sherwood Baptist and had become more active in a church than I had ever been.

About the only thing missing was a good girlfriend. Not just any girlfriend, though. What I wanted and needed was a *good* girlfriend.

Enter Ramona Hastings into the picture.

I had been interested in another young lady who was a freshman at Fort Valley State, about an hour-and-a-half drive away. Her father owned dry-cleaners stores in Atlanta—I presumed he was like the George Jefferson of Atlanta—and that meant she had some money, and that actually was one thing I desired in a girlfriend then.

But Ramona was a beautiful young lady I had noticed on campus, although she didn't appear to be rich. I had met Ramona in a Bible study group of which she was the president. I learned that she hadn't been a Christian very long and, although she was enthusiastic about the Bible, she didn't seem to have yet acquired a deep knowledge of God's Word. She was three years younger than me and having been in the army and lived the life I had to that point, she seemed a little too young and inexperienced. But we got to know each other as friends through the Bible studies, and one day she called me on the phone. Her car wasn't working, and I still had three cars I had bought during my street days. I wanted to help Ramona by loaning her a car, but I wanted to do it as a brother in Christ.

"Lord," I prayed, "please let me keep integrity in this situation here."

Sure enough, the more I was around Ramona, the more I liked her. And the more I was around Ramona, the more I realized George Jefferson's daughter at Fort Valley State wasn't right for me.

I called off things with the other girl.

"There's a young girl in our Bible study group," I told her, "and I'm liking her."

"Who?" she asked. "What witch is that?" (She actually used a not-nice word that rhymed with "witch.")

Her reaction confirmed that dating her would be settling for a girl who could have been a horrendous fit for the life I wanted to live in line with the calling God had for me. She wasn't a believer, and she didn't appear like she would become one soon. I had invited her to church several times, but she'd never gone with me.

"I think I like her," I repeated to her.

"You think?" she asked. "Does she like you?"

"I don't know. But to be honest about it, I think we should break things off."

Ramona had a strong personality, and I liked that. Too many of the girls I had dated had a "whatever you think" nature. Ramona, though, had strong, well-informed opinions.

I had typically greeted Ramona with a "brotherly hug"—the old side hug if you will—but as I sensed my feelings toward her moving in a more serious direction, I stopped hugging her. Ramona noticed and asked why.

"Well," I told her, "I'm interested in you as more than a sister in the Lord and want to respect you."

"Why didn't you tell me sooner?" Ramona shot back. "I've liked you for a long time!"

After a long history of making poor dating decisions, I finally made a good one when I decided to ask out Ramona.

Ramona had grown up in a black Baptist church, but she hadn't accepted Christ as her Savior until about a year earlier at a gospel concert on campus. I invited her to attend Sherwood Baptist with me, but she declined because of its reputation as being "a white church" and because she thought we should be attending a black church. She went back and prayed about my invitation and decided to visit Sherwood with me.

She immediately liked the church and its people, wound up getting baptized there, and joined me in getting involved with ministry in the church.

Ramona and I dated for two years. She graduated from Albany State in 1992 with a degree in biology. I received my political science degree a year later. After I graduated, in May of 1993, we married.

Ramona is my greatest treasure, what Proverbs 12:4 calls "an excellent wife" who "is the crown of her husband" (NKJV). I did not deserve such a good woman. When I asked her how in the world she could have become interested in me, she said, "Your empathy for people moves me. You have a lot of sympathy for people who have made mistakes and need to be loved anyway."

I consider Ramona the one filled with compassion because she knew all about my baggage—and there was plenty—and loved me anyway.

Answering the Call

Because I had received tuition assistance through the Reserve Officer Training Corps (ROTC), I owed the army additional service time after graduation. Two months after finishing up at Albany State, I reported to Fort Hood in Central Texas, where I became an infantry officer and, later, an aide to a four-star general.

I had felt a calling at various times back in high school, and I had finally kept my commitment to God the final time I enrolled at Albany State. But it was during my time at Fort Hood that everything seemed to come together for me spiritually, and I finally began to act on God's call on my life.

I often talked with the pastor of our church about my sense of being called into ministry. Through our discussions and our devotions and prayers together, I became sure that God desired that I enter full-time ministry. But I was a full-time soldier and expected to be asked to re-up when my military service was over. Plus, I was moving up in the military and thriving in the environment of competition for advancement.

God took care of both for me.

He placed me in a position to see different occurrences that chipped away at my level of satisfaction in the army, including witnessing how a couple of officers intent on working their way up the ladder had stepped on a couple of soldiers along the way. I am a competitive man, but I didn't want to be a part of any of that.

Then, in 1996, when it came time for my final performance review, my Professional Development Officer asked where I wanted to be in five years. I knew my response would determine my grade in the category of motivation.

"Sir," I replied in a voice that was a little weaker than I'd like to admit, "in five years, I want to be doing what God's telling me to do. Sir, I feel like since high school God has been calling me to the ministry, and I feel like, at this time, he has affirmed that. And so, in five years, I want to be doing what God's called me to do."

The colonel cussed in just about every other sentence when he talked. Surprisingly, he supported my plans and went out of his way to help me receive a discharge with an honorable and excellent performance rating.

My time in the military was to end in December 1996, but with the three months of leave I had built up, I was able to accept a job as a full-time youth pastor at Memorial Baptist Church in Killeen, the small city adjacent to Fort Hood, Texas.

I held that job for almost two years, and our daughter Gloria was born in Killeen. While I was a youth pastor, I began attending seminary. Southwestern Baptist Theological Seminary in Fort Worth,

Texas, has a satellite campus in San Antonio, and I made the two-and-a-half-hour drive to San Antonio on Mondays—my only day off because I ran our church's bus ministry on Saturdays—to begin working on a master's degree.

Taking those first classes confirmed the importance of earning a seminary degree, and Ramona, Gloria, and I moved to Fort Worth at the end of 1997 to attend Southwestern full-time. Ramona, who became a science teacher after we moved to Texas, took a teaching job at a middle school in the Fort Worth Independent School District. I also took a part-time position as a youth pastor at Cedar Cliff Baptist Church in Cedar Hill, south of Dallas.

When I started at Southwestern, I carried my books in one of those big tote bags with an over-the-shoulder strap. My bag was not stylish. In fact, it looked horrendous. But I was a southern Georgia boy. All I cared about was getting the job done—get my books to class, back to my car, and into my home—and my tote bag did that quite well, thank you very much.

I noticed my bag was different from the other students' bags, though. I remember one student who was a well-cut and handsome fellow. His father was pastor of a good-sized Baptist church in a Fort Worth suburb, and this student carried a nice-looking briefcase around campus. At the end of class, he would place his books in his briefcase, then shut and lock it with a distinctive *click-click*. I can still clearly hear in my mind.

Watching his routine one day, it dawned on me how different my zip-up tote bag was. My bag was so big that I could have loaded all my books plus his briefcase in my bag. Then maybe even my shoes.

A couple of weeks into classes, some of the students started making fun of my bag.

"Where are you traveling to today, Reese?" was a typical comment.

I was convinced the students were trying to be demeaning, but I laughed off their remarks. Believe me. I had heard much, much more demeaning remarks back in Georgia.

A friend named Charles Hewitt would take up for me in front of the teasers, and one day he brought a new briefcase he had bought for me. I appreciated the gesture, and I started using his gift in place of my big tote bag. But I didn't find the briefcase very practical. I couldn't fit all my books in it like I could in my tote bag, so instead of carrying all my books in one bag, I had to change out books according to what classes I had each day. Charles's gift was thoughtful, but it required that I become more organized!

My part-time position at our church didn't pay enough to cover my tuition and living expenses, so I took a part-time job at a gas station. One day I spotted a white customer struggling to operate a pump. When I walked over to the driver's side window to collect the man's money, I recognized him as a professor at my seminary. I was excited about being able to meet him. But instead of handing the money to me, the professor threw it out of the window to the ground and sped off.

I stood there stunned.

I wondered if he knew I was a student at his seminary. Then I realized it should not have mattered whether he had known I attended his school. I didn't know if he threw the money because I was black or if he had been in a hurry or angry or frustrated about the pump. My boss at the gas station, who was a white man and not a Christian, started calling the professor a jerk and other name and then bent over to pick up the money so I wouldn't have to.

I was not about to tell my boss that the man was a seminary professor, but I must say that at the time, I didn't disagree with some of the names my boss was calling the man. The professor did act like a jerk.

I also knew I was going to have to talk with the professor.

Dr. Martin Luther King Jr. once said, "No man can stand on top because he is put there." My Momma took that quote and revised it, telling me, "No man can stand on your back when you are standing up." I learned from both my Momma and my dad the importance of respectfully confronting people.

My dad had an eighth-grade education, but he was a math wizard—more so than most people would have expected. I remember one time when my dad was given the wrong amount of change by a white man in a store in what likely was not an honest mistake. "You didn't give me the right money," my dad confidently and respectfully informed the man. "Take this money back, and let's count it again."

My Momma would say, "You can look anyone in the eyes and tell them what you think, as long as it's in a godly way." Because of her advice, I did not grow up afraid of confronting anyone as long as I did so in the right spirit.

I made an appointment with the professor. After I introduced myself as a student, I asked if he buys gas at the station where I worked. When he said he did, I recounted what had happened. "You might have been in a rush or angry or frustrated with the pump," I told him, "but you made me feel like less of a human being, and I thought I needed to tell you that."

The professor immediately became sorrowful and asked, "Would you please accept my apology?" He was obviously humbled by what I had said, and I forgave him without a second thought.

I also told him that my boss was not a Christian, had witnessed the incident, and had said some unflattering things about him. I told the professor I did not think the things my boss said were true but that his actions had left me in a position where I couldn't defend him. The professor said he would go apologize to my boss, too. And he did. I gained a lot of respect for the professor, and we wound up having a great relationship during my time in seminary.

It's possible to speak and stand for the truth without creating conflict. Proverbs 15:1 says, "A soft answer turns away wrath, but a harsh word stirs up anger" (NKJV). In Ephesians 4:15, Paul talks about "speaking the truth in love." Later in that chapter, he also warns of the danger of becoming angry and *not* confronting our offender in a godly manner: "Be angry, and do not sin; do not let the sun go down on your wrath, nor give place to the devil" (Ephesians 4:26-27, NKJV).

    I imagine Paul would tell my Momma she gave me great advice.

Chapter 4

Saying Goodbye

There's nothing like a trip to the Caribbean to spark an interest in missions!

Dr. Dan Crawford, one of my professors, urged me to go on mission trips, and when an upcoming trip to the Caribbean was announced, I thought, *Why not? It can't be that bad serving God in a vacation spot!*

Except I didn't have the money to make the trip. I was no longer working at the gas station because our church had asked me to become the pastor, and all our income came from what pay-wise was a part-time job at the church and Ramona's teaching job. But the people of my church pitched in to help me, and Dr. Crawford also helped raise money for me to go.

Another seminary student and I flew into Grenada, and I spent most of the week with a national pastor on Union Island. The pastor's small church was holding a revival, and I was invited as a guest speaker. The church could hold sixty people jam-packed, so a loudspeaker was set up outside for the overflow crowd.

I kept telling God, *wow, You must really be preaching through me because I've never seen so many people wanting to hear me preach!* But then I learned why so many people were coming: they had never seen a black missionary.

I tried to convince the people that I wasn't technically a missionary, but when the pastor and I visited people and witnessed to them during the day, they would say to me, "You're that black missionary!" I would walk into a store to buy a Coca-Cola and be told, "You're the black missionary—the Coke is free."

Being called a missionary slightly agitated me because I wasn't one. I was a seminary student, and I did not think I should be afforded the same title and honor as official missionaries. But my efforts were fruitless, and I finally gave up on trying to convince the people otherwise and started going with the flow.

Toward the end of the week, a school asked me to speak and then have a question-and-answer session with students. As I spoke, I recognized a few of the local church members in the audience. During the Q&A, the adults raised their hands to ask me questions that allowed me to share the gospel. The pastor had planted the members in the audience for that very purpose!

I enjoyed ministering at Union Island, and as I was climbing the steps from the tarmac to board the plane, I sensed a question in my

Willing to Risk it All

mind: "Won't you be a missionary for Me?" I wasn't completely sure the question was from God, but it sure seemed like it.

When I returned home and informed Ramona that I thought God might be calling us to missions, she said, "You're crazy!" Neither one of us had seriously considered becoming missionaries. We thought God's plan for us was for me to finish seminary and remain at our church, which was growing and becoming more diverse as the community around us became more diverse. The church and community seemed to be a great fit for us, and we wanted to be part of even further growth for the church.

But I couldn't dismiss that question: "Won't you be a missionary for Me?"

After my trip to the Caribbean, Dr. Crawford informed me of a mission trip to China in three months. It was a prayer-walking trip, which involved walking through neighborhoods and praying for the Chinese people and for opportunities to share the gospel with them.

I asked Dr. Crawford about the cost.

"Twenty-one hundred dollars," he said.

I almost laughed. I had just come home from the other mission trip, which I had made only because of the generosity of other people. I told Dr. Crawford I would talk to Ramona, confident there was no way she would say yes.

"Reese," Ramona told me—she had started calling me Reese back in college because there was another Eric in our Bible study—"we've been poor all our lives. We are just now getting ahead to where we can pay the bills. We can't go into debt, but if you feel like God is calling you, then go."

Surprised at Ramona's openness to the idea, I told Dr. Crawford I could make the trip but added that I would only go if I could pay for the full amount upfront. I didn't want to create any debt to go. He told me the trip was with the Southern Baptist Convention's IMB, which had a special program that would pay for half of the cost for seminary students going on their first IMB mission trip.

Dr. Crawford, the seminary, our church, and friends got behind me again and covered the other half of the cost. They kicked in so much money that I had $400 of spending money for the trip.

I made four mission trips while I was in seminary, and God provided the money for each. I know I would not have been able to afford to go on even one of them on my own.

As the China trip neared, Dr. Jerry Rankin, the IMB president, spoke about missions in a Southwestern chapel service. When he asked at the end of his message for students to come forward for prayer if God was speaking to them about missions, I was one of the first to reach the front.

Dr. Rankin left the pulpit and came down among us students. He walked up to me and asked, "Brother, what is God telling you?"

I answered that I felt called to missions but that my wife did not sense the same calling.

"If I know God," Dr. Rankin said, "He will call her, too, so there is no need for you to worry."

I consulted Dr. Crawford about what Dr. Rankin said, and he told me not to put any pressure on Ramona. I didn't even tell her what happened in chapel, but I did begin to pray in earnest that she would receive the same word from the Lord that I was receiving if His will for us was to become missionaries.

Ramona: 'I'm Ready'
In China, not only did our team prayer-walk the neighborhoods, but I also visited a house church that met in secret. An elderly missionary woman led me to the meeting, and she discreetly pointed out their people who acted as "lookouts" to make sure police weren't following other believers or us.

It was freezing cold, and we were having to walk because the missionary did not own a car. On top of that, she had recently undergone back surgery. I couldn't believe this elderly woman with a bad back was walking through freezing temperatures, grimacing in pain occasionally, to attend a secret house church where, if the police found out about the meeting, she could be thrown in jail.

There were about a dozen people inside the small apartment, and I was amazed by how thrilled they seemed with having the opportunity to meet.

I had been invited to speak to the people, and they pulled out a small chair for me to sit in. I mean, that chair was tiny. I weighed about 250 or 260 pounds at the time, and I looked at that chair and prayed, *Oh, Jesus, I'm just too big. Please don't let it break!* I carefully lowered my backside onto the chair, slowly testing its ability to hold my weight. When the chair passed the test, I let out a sigh of relief. I couldn't have imagined how embarrassing it would have been for the special guest to break a chair. That was not the memory I wanted to leave behind!

The missionary was going to translate my message into Cantonese, but she first announced that she was going to sing a song in English. That immediately raised my curiosity because I didn't think anyone in the room other than me would understand what she was singing.

Then she began to sing,

'Tis so sweet to trust in Jesus,
Just to take Him at His Word...

Right there in front of everyone, smothering my undersized chair, I began to weep. The song was meant for me. I was prepared to speak about faith, but there I was struggling with trusting Jesus with my call to missions. As the elderly missionary woman wrapped up the song, I envisioned myself as a missionary.

As soon as we finished at the house church, I hustled back to my hotel and gathered our team members. I started bawling big time as I told them about my call to missions and how my wife hadn't received the same call. Everyone on the team kneeled and prayed for Ramona and me. When we finished, I went downstairs to the hotel desk and asked about the cost of a call back to the States. Thirty-five dollars for ten minutes, I was told. I paid the cost out of my spending money and called Ramona.

It was morning back in Texas, and Ramona had just completed her daily devotional. I told her that I had something to tell her, and she said she had something to tell me, too.

Being a properly brought-up man, it was lady first.

Ramona told me she had been reading Hebrews 10 the night before and that God had spoken to her throughout the entire chapter concerning her procrastinating praying about the call to missions I had received. God had revealed to her that she had not been praying because of the personal sacrifice she believed it would be to even consider becoming a missionary.

She read verse 38 to me: "Now the just shall live by faith; but if anyone draws back, My soul has no pleasure in him" (NKJV).

Ramona said she felt like God was saying to her, "Now, you can do whatever you want. But if you don't do this, I'm not going to be pleased with your life."

"I'm ready," Ramona told me.

Momma

In the spring of 1999, with me on schedule to graduate from Southwestern in December, Ramona and I got in touch with the IMB. We had no idea if the Board had black missionaries. After all, we had been around too many churches that did not welcome black Christians, and we considered it possible that a traditionally white denomination might not approve black missionaries. When we learned there were black missionaries in the IMB, we began to look at mission opportunities around the world.

We decided we would pray and, without consulting each other, pick three places each that interested us. We researched locations separately and didn't confer because we wanted God to show us in harmony where we should go.

When we compared our picks, I had written down China, Taiwan, and Rio de Janeiro. Ramona's three choices were all in South America. Rio was the only place we both had listed. After receiving approval from the IMB, we informed our church of our intentions. The church members were so kind to us because we gave what turned out to be a six-month notice that we would be leaving.

I had once given a two-month notice that I would be leaving a job, and that situation had turned out so badly that I decided a two-week notice would be the best route to go the rest of my life. But we didn't want to keep a secret from our church and went with honesty being the best policy. The people of Cedar Cliff received the news so graciously. They were proud for us and allowed us to stay on all the way through my graduation, at which point we would leave to begin seven weeks of IMB training.

I completed my Master of Divinity in December, and we returned to Georgia to see family for a couple of weeks before heading to Virginia and the IMB missionary learning center.

Momma had some health issues. She was a diabetic, and was on dialysis. But I was not prepared for the first time I saw her after graduating. She was sitting in a chair when I walked into the room, and I was horrified at how much weight she had lost and how skinny she had become. I sat at her legs, placed my head on her knees, and cried.

"Momma, what is going on?" I asked.

"Baby," she said, "this dialysis is causing me to lose weight and get really weak. I just can't eat much."

I wanted to stop crying but couldn't.

After a couple of minutes of leaning on her, I raised my head to look into her face.

"Momma, I'm going to be going to Brazil. God's called me to be a missionary."

"Okay, baby," Momma said. "I'm gonna be all right."

She rubbed the top of my head.

"I'm gonna be all right."

With our time to leave for training nearing, I received a phone call from my brother Clifford.

"Momma's been rushed to the hospital," he said. "She had a stroke."

She suffered three strokes. Momma could not speak, and I would visit her in the hospital, look at her, talk to her even though I knew she would not respond, and pray for her.

I prayed one night that Momma would get up out of that bed, and when I told Clifford, who had become a pastor, what I was praying, he said he'd had the same dream about her. But Momma wound up on life support, and we all had to face the decision of whether to leave her on life support or take her off. We brothers and sisters disagreed on how to proceed, and the doctor said he would leave her on life support unless all the siblings signed a notarized statement stating our agreement with removing her from life support. It took a while and a few discussions with doctors about her condition before we all reached the conclusion that Momma's time had come and the best thing for her would be to remove the life support.

Forty-eight hours after the doctors followed our wishes, on the day after Christmas, Momma was in heaven.

Almost a week later, still feeling numb from her passing, I preached Momma's funeral. Not all us kids were following Christ, and I knew that Momma would have wanted me to give an appeal in Jesus' name for them to return to God and the church. Three of my brothers wept during my message, and they decided to recommit their lives to Christ. Just as there had been during her life, there was fruit from my mother's death.

Like many young black men raised in fatherless homes, I owe much to a mother who prayed and persevered so I could make it to where I am today. Momma raised us on a shoestring. The psalmist must have had someone like my mother in mind when he wrote in Psalm 116:15, "Precious in the sight of the Lord is the death of His saints" (NKJV).

Momma often questioned herself as a mother and claimed that she had missed the mark at times. But if I could have one more conversation with her, I would tell her that considering all the factors, "You did a tremendous job. You took me to church, and because you did, I met Jesus. You never allowed us to see ourselves as poor and dumb, as uneducated. Thank you for that. You never allowed us to limit ourselves because of our income. Never. Thank you for that."

I remember one time after I had moved out of the house when I was sixteen, I was angry with Momma for not handling a situation with one of my sisters like I thought she should. Out of anger, I told her, "You are a poor excuse of a mom."

That was so untrue, and I hated myself for saying that to her. I told her I was wrong and that I should not have said that. But my words shook her. I felt like a creep for hurting Momma like that. I told her many times I was sorry, but it was an unfair comment that I could have never apologized enough times for saying.

Momma was a good mother, and all it takes is the death of a godly parent for a child to realize he didn't say "Thank you" near enough.

Chapter 5

Welcome to Rio

Rio de Janeiro is a city of stark contrasts.
On the one hand, it is like the 130-foot-tall *Cristo Redentor* ("Christ the Redeemer") statue overlooking the city: majestic, inspiring, arms opened wide to welcome all.

That is the Rio de Janeiro that visitors from around the world come to see, its stunning beaches and alluring nightlife attracting more tourists than any other South American city. That is the Rio that earned the right to host the World Cup and the Summer Olympics, with both awarded as nods to an economic surge in Brazil projected to elevate the country into the top tier of world economies. Along with its natural beauty, one of Rio's strongest assets is the warmth of its people.

But on the other hand, there is the Rio that our family lived and ministered in for seventeen years as missionaries. The city with the big statue and an image of welcoming people from all over had in some ways turned its back on its people.

That included the people who lived in the *favelas*, with no option but to live where homes were pieced together practically one on top of the other, and neighborhoods were often ruled by drug lords and controlled through fear. That also included the people among the hustle and bustle of the night-life districts, working in demeaning jobs they never would have chosen if they knew any other way to survive, or suffering through unfathomable hurts as they futilely attempted to find the love and acceptance missing from their lives.

Those are the people we pointed to the outstretched, welcoming arms of Christ the Redeemer—not the one placed on a pedestal and looking down on them from atop a hill, but the One who carried a cross up a hill for every one of them.

The opportunities were boundless in Rio. Imagine a city the size of Los Angeles, California, but with 2.9 million more residents than Los Angeles, and you have Rio de Janeiro. Add in the metropolitan areas surrounding the city, and there were more than 13 million residents. That was the mission field that became our adopted home. The people who lived there became our people.

I became the Mega-City Strategist in Rio for the IMB; the Southern Baptists, who have had missionaries in Rio for more than a hundred years, had four missionary couples in Rio at the time, with each responsible for different areas of ministry. My assignment was to work directly with the Brazilian national pastors in developing evangelism strategies.

Going into Rio, our emphasis was on reaching the members of the upper class because that traditionally had been the most difficult group to reach. But after we started working in Rio, God directed us to work with the urban poor. When we arrived, only 6 to 8 percent of Brazilians were considered evangelical Christians. In the *favelas*, the number likely was less than 1 percent.

Over time, we had to begin shifting more of our focus back to the upper class without letting go of what God is doing among the urban poor.

As Ramona and I look back on our time in Rio, we show God's plan strategically played out. On paper, it seemed like reaching the upper class first was the most effective strategy for evangelism. It turned out to be the opposite. The upper class and local, state, and national government officials became more accepting of us because of the tangible results they saw from God's work among the urban poor.

We also noticed an intriguing trend: the urban poor were much more effective at taking the gospel to the upper class than the upper class was at taking the gospel to the urban poor.

God used the urban poor—Rio's "least of these" in the eyes of some in the upper class—in a mighty way. For example, most of the upper-class families in Rio had maids who worked in their homes. The maids came from the urban poor, who worked in the city but lived in the *favelas* where we conducted much of our ministry. The maids in Rio often took on a child-rearing role in the homes where they worked, and Christian maids made a significant impact on the children of upper-class families.

God worked from the ground up, with the urban poor taking the gospel message into their jobs in the cities. Often, children were the point of entry for that message in reaching the homes of the upper class.

The evidence was all around us that nothing would fail faster than my strategies, and nothing would succeed faster than God's strategies.

Reaching the Urban Poor

What took place in the *favelas* of Rio was the same thing that has happened throughout the history of the church: where there is oppression, the church grows.

Some reports said as much as 22 percent of Rio's population lived in *favelas*. The *favelas* can't be broad brushed with statistics. The number of residents in a *favela* could range from 20,000 up to more than 150,000. Some *favelas* were contained in a small, flat area of land, while the larger ones ran up the surrounding mountainsides. Unemployment rates within a *favela* could be as low as 25 percent or as high as 75 percent.

Those fortunate to be employed, held jobs as maids, doormen, or gardeners. Most of their jobs paid minimum wage, and because Rio is a tourist city, the cost of living was high. Unable to purchase land, they lived in the shantytown-like *favelas*, where homes made of wood, tile bricks, or concrete were sardined into tiny spaces. The housing was not regulated.

Water, sanitation, and medical care were inadequate. *Favela* residents routinely died of such things as pneumonia or even a common cold. I was once told that 90 percent of people who lived in a *favela* died in a *favela*. Life expectancy in the slums was likely in the mid-fifties.

Ramona and I received a quick introduction to conditions in the slums when we first started ministering in our first assignment, Castle City.

Rodents were everywhere, dashing across the streets from trash pile to trash pile. Mangy dogs were lying in the streets waiting for someone to throw out scraps they could eat. Poop was everywhere, and the smell of raw sewage from the river gagged us. The small streets, most in poor condition, were clogged with motorcycles and pedestrians. Hundreds of wires hung across the streets, with most connecting to homes whose owners had tapped into the main wires so they could have electricity.

The later the hour grew at night, the louder the neighborhood became because of the music coming from clubs, people laughing and shouting in the streets, dogs barking, and motorcyclists honking their horns at residents walking into their paths.

When parents in *favelas* told us their hope for their children was that they could obtain an education, we learned that they were talking not about going to college but making it to high school. That was not easily accomplished. The parents wished they could afford to place their kids in a school where they could learn English, with the ability to speak English in Rio possibly meaning a step up in society through jobs tied into the tourism industry. Many times, learning English represented a kid's best chance of moving out of the slums.

The United States has poor inner-city neighborhoods with gangs, but those are nothing compared to Rio's *favelas*.

Discouragement overflowed in the *favelas*. Their residents had little hope. Yet despite that—or perhaps because of that lack of hope—the urban poor became Rio's most evangelized group. Our ministry worked in eighteen slums. The middle-class neighborhood that Ramona and I lived in was surrounded by three *favelas*. We lived within easy walking distance of the people who lived in those slums.

The *favelas* were filled with souls precious in God's sight. They were hardworking and humble people. A young woman Ramona was ministering to represented the mindset of those in Rio's slums. Talking about being born in the *favelas,* she told Ramona, *"Eu nasci para servir."* Translated: "I was born to serve."

Favela residents were very open and transparent, and they also were the people of Rio most receptive to the gospel.

The Southern Baptists had more church buildings and church members in *favelas* than among the upper class. That is one reason missionaries like Ramona, and I come back to the United States to raise money for missions. Our most reached people in Rio were the ones who could afford to build or independently sustain their own churches. We reached many people among the poor, yet we always had many, many more to reach.

The people of the *favelas* who attended church took their attendance seriously. I spoke with pastor friends back in the States who told me that when it rained, their church attendance could drop by half. When it comes to going to church, we Americans sure can be a bunch of bobos compared to the urban poor of Rio.

I knew many people in Rio who went to church when there were mudslides on the mountains—or even when it was raining bullets! *Favelas* typically were either controlled by drug cartels or paramilitary groups. It was not uncommon to be sitting in church and hear gunshots outside the church building. Still, church carried on, and people kept walking through the doors.

Always Protected

There was an odd dynamic within the *favelas*. The drug lords approved of someone like me who did good for the people of a community.

In the communities where they were in control, they ruled with surprisingly strict standards. The residents knew of the unforgivable acts, such as beating your wife, raping a child, robbing a person in the community, taking a picture of a drug-selling point, and ratting to the police.

Run afoul of those "laws," and you were dead.

Drug lords coveted order within their communities. They did not put up with locals doing anything that could bring a police presence into their territory. I had drug lords tell me, "Pastor, we've got to keep order in the community."

When they say they had to kill someone, they followed through. Yet, that renegade system of justice was all in the name of order because if someone committed an unforgivable crime according to their standards and got away with it, others could act outside of the rules, and order would be disrupted.

I heard the story of a city attorney and his wife who were carjacked by four young men from a drug-controlled community. The thugs pistol-whipped the man, stole the couple's car, money, and jewelry, and left the couple on a mountain road late at night. By community standards, the four young men were fine until they drove the stolen car into the community where they lived instead of abandoning it outside the community. Bringing the car into the *favela* brought the problem into the *favela*.

Television news stations aired stories about the robbery, and the top man of the community ordered the four robbers to be located and beaten. The one who had driven the car into the community was shot in each hand. One was shot in the leg, and another was shot in the shoulder. After justice was meted out against them, the four beaten men were loaded into a van and delivered to the hospital. The drug faction called the police to report at which hospital the men could be found.

The drug lord didn't want the police to come into his area to investigate the stolen car. In addition to taking care of the perpetrators, he also had the couple's jewelry taken to the police station along with the car—washed, vacuumed, and perfumed—so they could be returned to their owners.

A drug dealer once told me by way of introduction to his community, "Here's your rules, Mr. Preacher. The first rule is that drugs are never bad. The second rule is that drugs are never bad. The third rule is that drugs are never bad. And we have one other important rule: we don't mess with people who don't mess with us, and we only mess with people who mess with us. If you mess with us, we mess with you."

Pastors, typically, were highly respected. In addition to helping meet people's needs, we brought a spiritual presence into the communities. Even though the drug lords ignored God's standards that we preached, they respected the role the church played in Brazilian culture.

Some communities were run by paramilitary officials; usually, former policemen or military men who often had investments in the clubs in the *favela* and, thus, had self-serving incentives to keep order as they defined it in their communities.

On the surface, a paramilitary-run community sounds more desirable than one run by drug lords. But there can be corruption in these community "governments," if you will. It was not uncommon for paramilitary officials to charge "security fees" to local businesses to protect them. Funny how that worked out, but the business owners who did not pay for the protection were the ones most likely to have break-ins and other undesirable things happen to their businesses.

Another interesting thing was that being the top paramilitary official in a community could become an unenviable position. The top guy often lost his position at the same time he lost his life as the target of a drug lord or another paramilitary official looking to work his way up the power ladder.

But, as with some of the drug-run communities, we established working relationships with paramilitary leaders. Although the way leadership frequently changed within the communities, that could be a fluid process. Again, the Brazilians' respect for the church and pastors aided us in our mission to meet needs and bring a spiritual presence into the communities.

Having many different community leaders created an interesting work environment for a missionary. With the presence of warring factions within the communities, I not only had to remain neutral, but I also had to be careful not to create an impression that I had chosen sides. Complicating matters was that both sides were highly suspicious, to begin with. That was usually warranted because they had to be suspicious to survive.

For instance, I had to be careful about whose cell numbers I kept on my cell phone. If a member of the ruling drug lord's operation confiscated my cell phone and saw the phone number of the police chief, I could be killed as a police informant. I was diligent about deleting cell phone numbers I did not want to be caught with. As much as possible, when drug lords or chief paramilitary officers wanted to talk with me, I had them contact me through a third party. Or a fourth or fifth party, if possible.

I did not ask a lot of questions. I had a hardline stance against lying, which I will detail later, but I was going to be honest with people, and an honest "I don't know" often was the safest answer I could give. I wanted to maintain a reputation for being truthful, so when I said, "I don't know," a drug lord or a paramilitary official would believe that I did not know. Because I did not choose sides, I occasionally helped keep the peace between feuding factions. But ultimately, I was not in Rio to be a negotiator or a mediator. The only reason I went there was Jesus Christ. I was there to preach the gospel and bring people to Him by trying to help people see that Jesus makes a difference in lives.

Sometimes, I went out and ministered wearing a bullet-proof vest. Other times I chose not to because to take such a safety precaution could be seen as a betrayal of the trust I had built up with authorities in drug-dominated communities. If I wore a vest, they would view me as a double-crosser. But I always went out cloaked in the protection of God. Did that make me bulletproof? No, but there were instances when only God's protection enabled me to return home to my family.

And I know that part of God's protection was a praying wife. Let me tell you; my Ramona can pray. Almost every place in the *favelas* carried a risk factor. I monitored the risk levels of the various communities, and Ramona and our daughters—Gloria and Alicia (who was born in Campinas, São Paulo, almost four years after her sister was born—did not accompany me into areas that reached a certain risk level. But Ramona's prayers always went ahead of me and with me.

Ramona also taught our girls to pray for me. One night I overheard her in one of the girl's bedrooms telling them, "Let's pray for Daddy. He is going to a dangerous place tonight, and he needs our prayers." Then I would hear the three of them praying for God to protect me. That got to me every time. I knew Ramona and the girls were constantly praying for me. I didn't just know it. I felt it. Throughout the rest of this book, you'll read some of the prayers that Ramona recorded in her journals during our time in Rio.

There were nights—and early mornings—when I arrived home later than expected. Ramona, God bless her heart, learned to expect the unexpected. Many of those times, I walked into our home to see Ramona sitting there reading the Bible and praying for me. When she was not physically with me in ministry because we deemed an area too risky for her to accompany me, she spiritually partnered with me in ministry, praying not only for my protection but also that souls would be reached for Christ. After all, saving souls was the sole reason we went to Rio.

Before Ramona felt called to missions, she believed it would be a sacrifice to even consider becoming a missionary. I heard her say many times that during our first few years in Rio, she thought there were sacrifices that she had to make in being there. But she came to realize that compared to what Christ did on the cross, she had not made one single sacrifice. "There has been one sacrifice made, once and for all," she sensed God telling her, "and that's what Christ has done."

Ramona's specialty, other than prayer, is encouraging others. She loves to build relationships. She ministered to so many people in Rio who called her a mother figure in their lives. But even Ramona had to be careful.

Part of her ministry was among Rio's expanding middle class. As a mom taking kids to school and all their social activities, she had opportunities to build relationships with the unreached in that class, too. But she couldn't tell other moms at the girls' ballet class, for instance, about the work we were doing in the slums because our association with the urban poor could have resulted in her automatically being cut off from those in the higher classes.

The rap on the urban poor was that they were a bunch of *banjitos* or thieves. That was so unfair. One of the slums in Jacarepaguá is Cidade de Deus, which translated into English is "City of God." Yet if you lived in the City of God and were dark-skinned, forget about someone in a higher class hiring you to work for them. A dark-skinned person in Cidade de Deus could be the best maid or the best cook in Rio yet would not be able to secure a decent job. That was how poorly the upper class looked upon them, and sometimes our working with them prevented Ramona from being able to make more friends than she did.

One of my favorite expressions is, "Everyone has the same value at the foot of the cross."

We had a lot of work to do in getting the Brazilians to see that every person was a creation of God and that when Christ went to the cross, He went for the upper class, the middle class, *and* the urban poor.

Rio was a city whose people were crying out, *Can someone help me? Can someone show me a better way?* They were hungry for the hope, and the promise contained in the gospel, and shared that hope and revealed that promise to as many as we could.

No matter what the obstacles were, though, we were not going to stop preaching "Jesus saves" because the gospel needed to get to those people. I was not deterred by what the price of sharing that gospel there might have been for me, even if it was my life. Ramona and I decided early in our time in Brazil that we were going to stay until God either took us or told us to leave. (Although we were thrilled when it turned out to be the latter!)

Like other missionaries who worked in high-risk areas, I had to consider that the potential cost of obeying God's call on my life might be my life itself. I hugged my family and told them I loved them before heading out to minister in the slums, fully aware that might have been my last opportunity to hug them and express my love for them.

Because of Ramona and the girls, my greatest personal fear was that one day I would not return home, that I would go out and share the gospel and not come back.

Also, like other missionaries who worked in high-risk areas, I wrote a letter to my wife that was filed away by our missions board and would be given to her should my life end there. My letter encouraged Ramona to be strong and tell the girls that Daddy was going to miss them, and that God has a plan for them, too. I reminded Ramona in the letter that she would not be alone, that God would comfort her and keep her.

Because we ministered in one of the most dangerous spots in the world, people were interested in hearing my stories. Several media teams visited us in Rio to experience and make videos or write articles describing what went into answering God's call there. I can recall four near-death experiences that resulted from taking American media groups with me into the *favelas*.

As a result of those "exciting" stories, I sometimes was portrayed as a John Wayne-type missionary. That made me uncomfortable because the truth was that I had feet of clay. I had faults and weaknesses. I made mistakes. I questioned God's call on my life. I doubted my faith, and I came *this* close to calling it quits and going home on multiple occasions.

But I couldn't leave Rio, regardless of what staying there might one day cost me, because Jesus Christ gave His life for me. I owed it to Him to stay, and I owed it to the people of Rio who did not yet know Him.

From Ramona's prayer journal, while reading Hebrews 10:5-10:
"Here we are, Lord, we have come to do your will."

Chapter 6

Sense of Urgency

It's difficult to convey in the United States and other countries that enjoy wide-ranging freedom and liberty just how urgent the message of repentance and salvation became in the *favelas*. I worked under a heightened sense of urgency. For each person I talked with, I might have been the last person sent to share the gospel with them.

Take "The Godfather," for example. For a year, he had wanted to kill me. I had witnessed to a young lady who chose to accept Christ, and I later learned that she was one of The Godfather's girlfriends.

The Godfather was a legend around Rio as far as drug lords went because, after having survived assassination attempts and prison terms, he was nearing age forty. It was rare to find a drug lord in the slums beyond his early thirties. It was said that the only way to become an old drug lord was to be imprisoned.

When The Godfather's girlfriend became a Christian and quit

sleeping with him, he arranged to send me word that he wanted me dead. Nobody messed with The Godfather. As a result, I had to pull out of ministering in the community where he operated. But when a tragedy struck the community, I felt God leading me to minister there again. The good we had been able to do there had boosted my image among the people, and one of the top managers in the community wanted me to continue helping the residents there. Without my knowledge, he took my cause to The Godfather.

When the manager suggested that the community would be better off if I were allowed to enter without fearing a hit being executed on me, The Godfather changed his mind.

The Godfather and I wound up developing a close relationship. He asked me to meet with him a few times about needs within the community. During those meetings, I began to share the gospel with him, and he was surprisingly interested in what I had to say. That led to him requesting monthly meetings with me, and as I built up trust with him, he granted me unprecedented access into his community.

Even when I received access into communities, there were designated areas I knew were off-limits. But there were no limits with The Godfather— not even the places where his operation stockpiled weapons and ammunition.

He once asked if I would pray over his weapons. I declined. "But I'll pray for *you*," I offered.

An I'll-scratch-your-back-if-you'll-scratch-my-back system was very much at work within the *favelas*. I had been scratching The

Godfather's back by helping the people in his community, thus helping keep order, and I developed an itch I thought I could use a good scratch in return.

We obviously needed to employ non-traditional methods of evangelism where we ministered, and sometimes when word got back to the States that I had been hanging out with drug lords—as if that were an accurate description—our methods could understandably be questioned. Thus, I asked The Godfather if he would consent to be interviewed by a small group from the IMB for a video that would describe how our ministry was making a difference in the lives of the people of Rio.

"Godfather, this is for me," I said. "I'm asking a favor of you because we have people in the States who don't know how to pray for these people. They don't know the reality we work in."

I was relieved that he didn't laugh and say no right away, but he didn't immediately sign on, either.

"I can guarantee that this will mostly be shown in churches in the States," I added.

He nodded that he would grant an interview, and one of his three stunned lieutenants listening in interrupted, "Wait a minute!"

The Godfather repeated that he would do the interview. But, he added, "I'm going to put on a mask, and I'm going to have my boys locked and loaded."

"Please," I responded, "because it'll be shown in churches, don't show the weapons."

"I'll tell you what," he countered. "Their weapons will be in their uniforms and out of sight of the cameras, but I've got to be able to defend myself—not necessarily from you and your men, but from anybody who might try to come in and rush us."

The drug cartels needed to be suspicious of everyone . In addition to legal forces that could decide to come in and clean out an operation, rival cartels wanted to expand their operations into others' territories.

Weeks ahead of the interview, I had to submit photographs of the four men who would be accompanying me, their names, their jobs, and the questions The Godfather would be asked.

The video crew scheduled two days of filming in the *favelas*. We would interview The Godfather on the second night.

Before leaving for the interview, we were eating at a mall—well, I wasn't eating because my stomach was in knots with nervousness—when I sent a text to the number three man in the operation to receive instructions on where to meet The Godfather.

"You'll be responsible for the guys that come," a text came back.

I replied that I understood.

I was told the destination and then that when we reached a point two miles out from the site, the other men were to close their eyes and keep them closed so that they could not identify the location and possibly report later to the police or a rival drug gang where we had met. Also, I was to bring a fresh batch of pictures of the men.

That last part put me into scramble mode. I located a bookstore in the mall where I could use a computer to access and print photos of the men from my Facebook account.

After nightfall, we set out in my pickup truck toward the meeting place. Two miles from our destination, I told the men to close their eyes and, no matter what, keep them shut until told otherwise.

The windows of my truck were rolled down, and I instructed the crew members to put their hands either on the door or on the seat in plain view.

Then I began to get nervous because I knew there would be spotters who would have radioed ahead that we had entered the zone. If we did not arrive in the amount of time they thought we should arrive, they would become suspicious of us, and that could mean big trouble.

Normally, I am a talkative guy. But that night, I didn't say much of anything because I was so focused on watching the surroundings as I drove. All kinds of danger lurked in the dark. The men were quiet, too. They didn't need to tell me they were scared; I could feel it inside the truck cab.

After driving two miles, I turned off the road and onto the grass. I tapped my horn twice as instructed. A wooden gate opened, and I drove slowly through the opening. Once we were inside, the gate closed behind us.

"My God," I said.

A masked man had walked up to the front passenger window and pointed his AK-47 to the side of the head of Brad, one of the crew's videographers who still had his eyes closed as ordered.

Another man, wearing dark clothes, gloves, and a ski mask, emerged from the darkness and walked up to my window from the front left of the truck.

He was the number three man I had been texting. He asked for the photos of the men, and I handed them to him. He had the original set of photos I had earlier sent him, and he started flipping through the pictures. He stopped at one of Steve.

And then he started angrily slapping the photo with his hand.

"*Que isso?*" he demanded. "*Que isso*" (What is this?)

He pointed to Brad's face on the photo. Brad had a beard in the photo, but he sat clean-shaven in my truck.

In Portuguese, I answered that Brad wasn't a Russian spy because some of the drug lords in Rio believed Russians were working with Americans to wipe out the drug operations.

I told Brad to open his eyes so the number three guy could get a better look at him.

"*Vire a direita,*" the man said, wanting me to tell Brad to turn his face to the right.

"*Vire a direita!*" I said to Brad.

Brad didn't move.

"*Vire a direita!*" I repeated to him, frustrated he hadn't done as told the first time.

The bodyguards around us started laughing.

"Pastor," the number three man told me in Portuguese, touching me with a .380 pistol, "you need to tell him in English."

I was so intense that I had been ordering Brad to face to the right in Portuguese. The bodyguards' laughter lightened the moment, but still, I was concerned that just by having an outdated photo, I had violated The Godfather's trust to the point that he would call off the interview.

"Please turn to the right," I said to Brad.

Brad looked to the right, and several times the man looked at Brad's picture and then to his face.

"It's okay," the man told me. "Now we're going to have to check you, Pastor."

"Okay, guys," I told the crew, "we're going to get out of the truck, and they're going to shake us down."

There was a makeshift shack ahead of us, and I thought I saw The Godfather sitting there, waiting for us. I wanted to call out to him that we hadn't backstabbed him and that the men with me knew the deal we had coming in. But before I could, the men in ski masks began frisking us. We were giving a frisking that, let's just say, was very thorough. I'll stop the description there.

Finally, the men were cleared to take their video equipment out of the truck and set up for the interview.

The Godfather was sitting at a small table in the shack, wearing a ski mask as he had said he would. The crew quickly set up its cameras and lights to focus on The Godfather. We knew going in our time would be limited, so not a minute could be wasted.

"Guys," I said at one point, "don't look behind you." I had told the crew not to video any weapons. "There are 9mm handguns pointed at us right now. Don't make any quick moves. Any quick moves, and we might not be here tomorrow."

I prayed they followed my instructions. When Americans came to Rio to work with me, they tended to do what I told them not to do. This was one time when all my directions absolutely must be followed to a T.

When the cameras and lights were trained on The Godfather, and we were ready to begin, he stood. Something wasn't right. He was noticeably taller. When Tristan, the interviewer, asked the first question, what we thought was the head bodyguard off to our right answered the question. *He* was The Godfather.

Brad adjusted a light to shine it on The Godfather, and my heart dropped. We didn't need to be moving anything without first receiving permission.

I would be interpreting the questions and answers, and I started to move closer to Tristan and the microphone. But I thought about the cameras and lights that could be moved and decided to stay farther back to make sure nothing crazy happened with the equipment.

The Godfather, wearing a black jacket, jeans, black gloves, and a black ski mask, stood with his back to the camera throughout the interview.

When asked to describe what it was like to be a powerful man in his community, he answered, "It's complicated. For you to be the boss in charge of a community, you need to respect to be respected. You need to respect the older people and the children because it is not the fault of old people and the children that someone must be in charge. It's for their welfare."

When Tristan asked The Godfather why he had allowed me to share the gospel with him, I choked up interpreting his answer.

"Pastor Eric came to the community, and everybody needs help in the community," he said. "Pastor Eric came to the community, and he didn't bring money, he didn't bring finances—he brought the love of God and a piece of God to us.

I had never heard The Godfather speak of me in that way. I had no idea that I'd had that kind of impact on the man who had once wanted me killed.

But then he answered a subsequent question in a way that made me cringe.

"We have to kill people now!" The Godfather said. "Those people who want to do bad things—to me—they are like trees that don't give good fruit. Like in the Bible. When you cut down this tree, you stop it from making the other trees bad. So, we have to kill some people. This is what I believe about how God works."

I knew that answer would have to be edited out of the video! I'd been sharing with The Godfather what the Bible says, but I clearly still had work to do.

Near the end of our allotted ten minutes, we heard a couple of gun fires in the distance.

"Okay," the number three guy said, "we've got to get y'all the hell out of here."

I didn't interpret word for word to the crew.

"He said it's time to go," I told them.

Then we heard more gunfire that sounded closer. The Godfather's men, afraid a rival drug lord's men might rush the interview, cocked their weapons, and pointed into the darkness.

The men in the crew began hurriedly packing their equipment. But they weren't hurrying enough by my preferences.

"Let's go!" I ordered them. "Do you hear the gunfire? Let's go, man! Somebody could be coming around that wall trying to kill us or be coming after The Godfather, and we'll get killed as innocent bystanders!"

That put a little extra hop in their steps until I spotted one of the men folding a piece of equipment. I had no idea what he was folding or how important it was, but I shouted at him, "Get in the freaking truck and stop trying to put stuff in all nice and neat! Throw it in the truck, and let's get out of here!"

We finally got all the gear and the crew members into the truck, and I ordered them to close their eyes again as we pulled back onto the main road. I provided the men a play-by-play description as armed men on motorcycles tailed us until we were out of their zone. At that point, I told the men they could open their eyes.

Some of their eyes were big from the experience. We laughed in the manner men do after just undergoing a major adrenaline rush.

That's when I informed Brad that when we had first pulled into the gate and I exclaimed, "My God!" one of The Godfather's men had the bad-boy end of an AK-47 a foot from the side of his head.

I told the men that if one of them had opened his eyes and seen the AK-47, he would not have been able to keep from reacting. But because they hadn't opened their eyes, the Godfather's men knew they were following orders and could be trusted.

The crew returned home to the States and produced their video. I continued to meet with The Godfather and share the gospel with him.

About seven months after the interview, The Godfather was assassinated by one of his many rivals. He let his guard down one night when he went to a club, and when he exited the building, rivals were waiting for him and shot him up along with three of his bodyguards.

Exactly three weeks earlier, I had spent time with The Godfather, we prayed, and he said he had accepted Jesus Christ as his Savior.

Becoming 'Known'

As in drug-run *favelas*, there were certain rules in paramilitary-run communities that resulted in major consequences when broken. Smoking marijuana, snorting cocaine, robbing, or injuring a store owner, and raping a child were offenses punishable by execution, with the offender's body thrown onto the main street or into an *esgoto* (an open sewage "lake") for residents to see. That was done all in the name of maintaining order.

Within this evil system, there were "good" rules for the residents to live by, such as take care of your family and be a father to your children, don't go out and get drunk, and dress yourself up and look presentable. But it could be very much a "do as I say and not as I do" setup, because the paramilitary leader who would make a public example out of you when he found out you had beat your wife might have ten wives himself.

A man named Gary had committed acts that threatened that order in one community, and one of the paramilitary leaders—whom I did not know, but the paramilitary had been keeping an eye on me without my knowledge—called and asked if I would visit with Gary.

I went to Gary's house and knocked on his door, and a man about my age answered. Gary invited me in, and I presented the gospel to him.

Gary told me he was a religious man. I asked, "If you were to die today and God asked you, 'Why should I let you into heaven?' what would you say?" Gary answered that he was a good employee, he didn't steal, he didn't smoke—although he did drink alcohol some—and he had not killed anyone. In his eyes, compared to what he had seen from others in the *favelas*, he considered himself "good enough" to earn entrance into heaven.

I agreed with Gary that being good was honorable but informed him that there was only one way into heaven, and it wasn't by being good. "In John 14:6," I explained, "Jesus Christ says that He is the way, the truth, and the life, and no one comes to the Father except through Him."

Gary, however, wasn't ready to accept that truth.

Later that day, a paramilitary official asked if I had spoken with Gary. I had, I told him. The official didn't ask anything about our meeting.

The next morning, I received another call on my cell phone requesting that I speak with Gary again. "He has become known in the community," I was informed. Becoming known in the community was a bad thing for an individual.

It was a Saturday, and because I had planned to spend the day with my family, I asked if I could wait until early the next week. It was strongly suggested that I not wait. Wanting to keep open the valuable lines of communication I established with the community's leaders, I agreed to visit Gary that day.

Again, I went to his house. This time, his wife answered the door. One of her eyes was dark and swollen. When she turned at an angle, I could see the other side of her face also was swollen. A girl about seven years old was hiding behind her mother, and when she poked her head around for a curious look at me, her red eyes revealed she had been crying. Gary came to the door, obviously drunk, and said he did not want to talk with me.

"Gary," I said, "it would be really good for you if we talked right now."

"Why?" he asked.

I told him about my phone call that morning and, in a loud voice, told him, "Sir, you've been made known in the community."

Horrified looks swept across both Gary's and his wife's faces. They understood his violation of the paramilitary's community standards had become known to the officials. His wife immediately stepped aside for me to enter. Gary sat in a chair, and I took a seat on the couch across from him.

"Listen," he began with a harsh tone, "I don't like Christians like you who try to force their religion down the throats of other people. That is not respectful, and it offends me!"

"Have I said anything about Jesus to you today?" I countered.

A disgusted look creased his face. "Now you're acting like I'm stupid, which is also offensive to me! Why would a preacher like you be here if you were not going to talk about Jesus?"

"Well, my friend," I said, "you are partially correct. But I want to talk to you today about mercy and grace."

"Listen to him," the wife timidly inserted.

Gary turned toward her and shouted, "Get out of here!"

His wife and daughter left the room.

I began to tell Gary the story from John 8 about the adulteress woman who had been brought before Jesus. "Jesus had mercy on her when she confessed humbly that the accusation was true. He told those around Him that if anyone was without sin, he should cast the first stone. Of course, no one was there who hadn't sinned, so those accusing her left. Jesus forgave that woman and told her not to sin anymore. She accepted God's grace."

I looked directly into Gary's eyes.

"It appears that someone has hurt your wife, and when I listened to how you talked to your wife and child a moment ago, it made me sad. I don't know what's going on in your marriage, but obviously, your wife loves you because she wants you to get help. God can change your marriage and you. I'm not talking about religion or denominations."

Gary stood up and shouted, "I've had enough! You have no respect for me and my house, and I am the man of my house!"

"I ask your forgiveness if I have said anything that gave you the impression that I do not respect a man's role as the leader of his home," I said. "Before I leave, can I pray for you?"

"No!" he snapped.

I left his home and had no additional contact with Gary.

Four months later, a friend asked if I planned to go into that same community that day.

"There's a dead man in the street whose body has been there all night," my friend told me. "If you want to minister to his family, you should go now."

My friend and I left for the community, and when we arrived at the scene of the body, I was saddened to see it was Gary's. His wife was there, and I asked what had happened. She told me Gary had come home late the night before, changed clothes, and left again. He had become so drunk at one of the bars that he made a pass at a woman. The bar owner called community leaders, and the only thing she knew from there was that her husband was found dead in the street.

Gary had violated what kept order in his community, and it cost him his life. I had never been afforded the chance to pray with Gary, and as far as I knew, no one else had either.

'How Long?'

With a team of twenty-five young people, we entered the community of Canal Vale to hold an evangelism event for children. We arrived well before the start time, finalized plans, and set up our equipment.

As the young people completed the preparations, I began walking around the area to pray and check for any security concerns. I noticed a wooded area about a hundred yards from where the event would take place, and as I continued to walk and put my military training into use to scan the area, I sensed movement within the trees.

My uneasy feeling remained as the event began, and I continued to walk, pray, and watch. My concern grew as the event progressed to the point that I dropped to my knees and began praying beside a burned-out truck positioned between the event and the woods. I stationed myself there, hoping that if there were people in the woods, they would see (and hear) me praying and either stay in the trees or leave.

I know for certain that two people saw me praying. The two drunk guys wobbled up next to me and asked if I was all right. One of them reached down to help me up, which was a bigger chore than he probably expected because not only am I a large man, but I also had bad knees from my football and military days.

"Hey, you're that American preacher!" one exclaimed. "Your preaching is really helping me, man!"

Then he grabbed me and gave me a big hug. If he hadn't been holding me so tightly, the smell of the alcohol on his breath might have knocked me over. Considering his inebriated condition, I wondered how effective my preaching had been.

"Well, praise God!" I told him anyway.

On the platform, the local pastor was wrapping up his message before the children performed a choreographed dance. The drunks kept talking to me, and I assumed the task of keeping them away from the event. Over the men's shoulders, I saw more movement in the wooded area. I called out to a team member to alert her, and that was all she needed to spring into action.

"Let's pack up!" she cried out. When that dear woman got to moving, you were better off not being in her path because there was no stopping her.

In exactly twelve minutes, we had all the equipment packed into the trailer behind my truck. We considered taking all the young people into the public restrooms for protection but quickly decided it better to get out of Dodge. Fifteen of our team members piled into our van, and the rest jumped into the back of my truck.

When we reached the bridge exiting the slum, a man with an AK-47 stopped us. I leaned my head out of the window. "*Calma, calma,*" I said to him to keep things calm. "We have just finished a children's program, and we are leaving now. I am a pastor."

The man cocked his assault rifle.

"How do I know that you don't have police in the back of the trailer?" he asked, pointing the gun at one of our young women who sat in the passenger seat.

I suggested the man call the Canal Vale manager, who could vouch for me. Instead, the man lowered his gun and ordered us to leave. Two hours later, a massive police invasion hit that slum. Thirteen people were killed. Six were authorities in the community, including the manager.

The next day, I returned to Canal Vale to comfort the families of those killed. I offered to preach funerals, but all the dead were buried without funerals within twenty-four hours.

One of the victims was a young teenager caught up in the shootout. One reason there was so much fear in the *favelas* was that innocent people often were shot in the crossfire. The teen's family lived in a shack on the outskirts of the community, and as I approached, his distraught mother came running out to me. "How long?" she cried out to me. "How long shall we live in situations with people like this dying daily? Can you ask your God that? Can you tell me how long?"

I asked if we could sit down. I had no direct answer to her questions.

"There was a man named Job," I told her, "who lost his family and everything in one day, but he still loved God. When his wife asked him, 'Why don't you just curse God and die?' Job still loved God. It's okay to ask God, 'How long?'"

As we continued to talk, I asked if she had ever accepted Jesus. The woman was a spiritualist, someone who believed that dead ancestors or saints could communicate with the living. I began to tell the spiritualist about God's *Holy* Spirit. That intrigued her. After I told her more about the Holy Spirit, I said, "Ma'am, I believe that if you allow God into your life, *He* can answer all your questions." Right there, we prayed, and she asked God to take control of her life.

The tensions remained around Canal Vale, and three days later, another shootout broke out. A stray bullet struck the mother in her head and killed her.

I couldn't help but think that God had sent me to the mother in her very hour of need because He knew what evil men would do only three days later.

Living and working in the slums of Rio made 2 Corinthians 6:2 even more real to me: "For He says: 'In an acceptable time I have heard you, and in the day of salvation I have helped you.' Behold, now is the accepted time; behold, now is the day of salvation" (NKJV).

People in the *favelas* grasped their mortality. As a missionary called to share the gospel with them, I grasped their mortality, too, and that gave me a sense of urgency. I was so serious about sharing Jesus with people there, and I was so afraid that God would hold me accountable for someone who died without me first sharing the gospel with them. That thought petrified me at times.

I often wondered how many more people back in the United

States would readily accept the gospel if we sensed a greater risk of dying? And, if we considered more each other's mortality, how many more people would readily *share* the gospel as we all are called to do? And thinking about how we don't do that now petrifies me, too.

From Ramona's prayer journal:
"Father, this is an acceptable time. We hear you, Lord. You have helped us, and we are saved. Thank You, Lord! Now, oh Lord, is the acceptable time for these people, too. Now is the day of salvation for so many of them who don't know You yet, Lord. Save, save, save the *Cariocas* living and working in the *favelas* of Rio. In the name of Jesus, I pray."

Chapter 7

Loving the Unlovely

Our claim to be Christians was never tested as seriously as when we were called to love the unlovely.

I love everything about Jesus, but I especially love how He embraced the unlovely of His day, such as tax collectors, prostitutes, lepers, and social outcasts. Jesus ministered to people the religious establishment wouldn't touch, and I also love how He didn't mind that the establishment became upset with Him for associating with those needy people.

We established what we called "Care Night" in Rio when our ministry team went into the busy nightlife districts and ministered to the unlovely of our city—those who weren't cared for by Rio's daytime world. Care Nights excited me because if there was one thing the people we talked to on the streets needed most, it was love. My calling from God was to make sure they were enveloped with as much love as God could give through our team and me.

Prostitution was legal in Brazil for ages 18 and older. The Ministry of Labor listed "sex worker" as a legitimate occupation, which granted prostitutes the right to receive a pension and benefits from the government when they retired. Prostitution made a significant contribution to Brazil's economy. Although operating a brothel was illegal, the law permitted the operation of hotel bars, massage houses, and similar places where prostitutes could work.

We understood the country's sex laws would not change, but we could work to change the lives of those working in the sex industry.

That's where Care Night came in.

Each Tuesday and Thursday, our team gathered at our house at 11 p.m. for a devotional and to pray for our Care Night. We knew we would encounter people who lived in physical and spiritual darkness, and we asked God to demonstrate to them His love so they could be brought into His kingdom of light. Around midnight, we left for the streets crowded by those working in Rio's famed nightlife.

We regularly ministered in the Flamengo district, a beachfront area on the edge of Guanabara Bay. Flamengo was a neighborhood in transition. Historically, it had been a seedy part of Rio, with all kinds of sinful temptations. Recent efforts had attempted to transform the area into a social scene with clubs and restaurants for young adults, and that resulted in an increase in the number of middle- and upper-class college students and other young people in their twenties hanging out there. But Flamengo also had designated areas where prostitutes and transvestites peddled their services on the streets.

Our team typically split into pairs in Flamengo, and one night I set out with Sam, a student missionary working with us for the summer.

As we walked toward one of the transvestites' areas, Sam grew less talkative and increasingly tense looking. Most Americans who came down to work with our team for short terms had never seen a transvestite, much less talked with one. Sam belonged in that category.

I spotted "Jennifer," a transvestite I had known for about two years. Brazilians' customary greeting is a kiss on the cheeks, although it's more like touching cheek to cheek while giving "air kisses."

I walked up to Jennifer, and we greeted in typical Brazilian fashion. Then I introduced Sam to Jennifer. When Jennifer stepped toward Sam to greet him with a kiss on the cheek, too, Sam pulled back. "No, no," Sam said before turning away.

Three other transvestites working the same area watched with offended facial expressions as Sam walked off. I was embarrassed and apologized to the "ladies." Not wanting to lose an opportunity to minister to them—that night and potentially in the future—I immediately engaged my friend Jennifer in a conversation.

"How are things going with you?"

"Miserable," Jennifer said.

Another transvestite joined in, pointing toward Sam off in the distance. "What he just did to us is how we feel treated by society. And that is why we do this at night."

"What that guy did," another added, "is why many of us don't believe in God. God is not love if you who call yourselves Christians treat us that way."

Stinging words to hear, for sure, but the door had been opened for me to say, "The standard of love is not my friend or me. The standard is what Jesus did for you on the cross."

"I'm tired of this," one of the transvestites shot back. "Can you move over a little? I need to stand out here in the street to make money. Don't talk to me no more."

One of Jennifer's friends wanted to ask me a question.

"I was in a church, and I know who Christ is," said "April," dressed in a short skirt and a revealing top and wearing a wig. "But you know what? I went to my pastor and talked to him about my feelings toward men. Two Sundays later, he preached against homosexuality, saying that God was going to destroy and kill all those types of evil spirits just like he did with Sodom and Gomorrah."

April's eyes revealed pain as the story progressed. The Holy Spirit seemed to be telling me that April didn't want to be working on the streets but was acting out in anger.

Jennifer walked away, and I moved over to a place where I could sit down. I motioned for April to join me.

"What do you think of me?" I asked. "Have you seen me come down here before?"

April acknowledged seeing me.

Jennifer was still nearby, and I called out, "Jennifer, have I ever treated you badly during the two years I've known you?"

"No way!" Jennifer quickly responded.

"Have I ever spoke to you in a condemning way?"

"No," Jennifer said, easing nearer to us.

"Have I given you a Bible before?"

"Yeah, and I still have it."

"Have I talked to you about the love of God?"

"Yes."

"Okay, thank you."

Jennifer then left April and me alone again.

"Man is imperfect, but God is perfect," I continued. "His love is unconditional. We don't have to meet any conditions beforehand to receive His perfect love."

Tears flowed down April's angled, makeup-covered cheeks. I sensed the Holy Spirit telling me to give the transvestite a hug.

No way! I thought. *That wouldn't look good. That is an appearance of evil!*

The tears continued, and so did the Holy Spirit's prompting of me.

I kept resisting until it struck me like a two-by-four across the forehead that my resistance made me no different than Sam.

April looked up at me, eyes filled with tears. "You know, when I went to that pastor, I wanted to hear what you just said."

In my soul, I kept debating with the Holy Spirit.

"All I wanted was to be accepted, love, and helped," April continued. "I knew that my feelings for men were wrong. I was fighting those feelings. That's why I went to my pastor. I have told only two people this besides you—my mother, who didn't believe me, and one of my transvestite friends, who did believe me. I'm twenty-eight years old. From age nine to sixteen, my stepfather sexually abused me. He was supposed to be a Christian and attended church. When I went to my pastor, I was going to confide in him about what my stepfather was doing, but he never gave me a chance. So that Sunday, two weeks later, when he preached against homosexuality and suggested that I had an evil spirit, I stood up and walked out of that church. I don't enjoy selling myself like this. Just to be able to do it, I have to be high or drunk."

The transvestite's crying turned to sobbing. I could no longer resist what the Holy Spirit wanted me to do. I reached over and embraced the man. It was a short embrace, but as we hugged, I said softly, "Jesus loves you, this I know."

April stood up, with body posture suggesting all the emotion that had poured out had left the transvestite drained.

"I'm going home," April said. "I can't be on the streets tonight."

"Can I give you something to read?" I asked.

April nodded and took a gospel tract on peace written by Billy Graham. "Thousands of people have come to know God as their Savior because of the ministry of this man," I said and then handed over my business card.

"I know of a ministry that has a house for transvestites wanting to leave that way of life. If you call me, I can guarantee you a place in that house."

The transvestite thanked me, turned, and walked away.

Sam, unbeknownst to me, had been observing our entire conversation from a distance.

After we had wrapped up our Care Night, Sam and I returned to my truck. Sam didn't say a word as I drove toward home. I broke the silence.

"Sam, ministry is not about us. It's about Jesus. I'm not going to get on to you for what you did. I had my own struggle tonight about hugging a transvestite. Jesus' hands were nailed to the cross. So were His feet. His side was pierced. So, what is it for me to slide over and give that transvestite a hug?"

Silence returned to the truck. I couldn't help but cry as I realized a valuable lesson about loving the unlovable had been taught that night—and *I* had learned it.

From Oldest Profession to New Creation

One thing certain about ministering to prostitutes was that it could be unpredictable.

A pastor friend from the States came down to minister with us, and I took him out for a Care Night. We were sharing with a prostitute about Jesus when, catching us completely off guard, she lifted her shirt, completely exposing herself to us.

My friend and I immediately looked away. His jaw plummeted down toward his chest, and his eyes exploded to as big as saucers. I knew the enemy had created that distraction, and we halted the conversation with the prostitute.

My pastor friend was visibly shaken, and he later told me it took him a couple of weeks to get the image out of his mind. I had recovered rapidly. Even though I had been stunned by the prostitute's action, I had learned to expect the unexpected in Rio.

Copacabana was another area we ministered in during Care Night. Think Bourbon Street in the French Quarter of New Orleans, but bigger, louder, crazier, and more spread out, and that was the Copacabana district. Once the area reached the fully hopping level at night, usually around midnight, the bars, clubs, strip joints, discotheques, and the sidewalks that connected them teemed with people. Many of the businessmen coming into Rio from all over the world chose to go into the district on the south side of the city at the end of their day. Copacabana was one giant temptation, from start to finish.

There was the main road through Copacabana. One side had an open-air market we would see tourists shopping in. On the other side of the street, we would see a patio bar filled with international businessmen checking out the prostitutes working their way through the crowd as they tried to attract customers. Once a prostitute's rate was negotiated and her official HIV-negative certificate shown, she and her client disappeared into the hotel's bar. It was as accepted as paying a plumber or electrician to make a repair.

Sex was a product available anywhere and anytime for the right price.

A member of our ministry team knew all too well how the sex business worked. Before becoming a Christian, she worked as a prostitute. She shared with us the many different pains the prostitutes suffered through. Heartache, emptiness, disease, shame, fear, abuse, loneliness—the list grows long. For most, prostitution was a means of survival. It was the only way they could make the money they needed or wanted.

Much as with the order-keeping rules of the drug lords and paramilitary officials in the *favelas*, the prostitutes established their own unwritten rules to respect and follow. One rule was not to cross into each other's territory. The streets or areas were divided up and crossing the line into someone else's area could come with a price because many of the prostitutes carried a knife, a box cutter, or, in some cases, a gun.

On one Care Night, our team was walking the district sharing the gospel with any prostitute who would stop soliciting potential customers long enough to listen. Yelling and screaming from a nearby group of prostitutes caught my attention.

One of the women was shouting at me.

"Pastor! You know the rules! This girl is breaking the rules. She's working *our* street!"

The prostitutes protecting their area had surrounded the young blonde girl, who was so overcome with fear that she was crying and shaking.

"Pastor," another prostitute exclaimed as I slipped my way inside their circle, "this girl needs Jesus because she's getting ready to meet Him!"

The alleged rule-breaker, I later learned, was only nineteen years old. She apparently was new to the business, too, because she shouted back to the others, "This is Rio de Janeiro, and no one owns any street! I can stand and work wherever I want."

Wrong answer.

One of the women reached around me to slap the young blonde.

"Stop it!" I told the slapper. "Don't hit people!"

Another prostitute grabbed the blonde's purse and tossed its contents into the street. That got the group worked up even more.

You probably wouldn't think it possible unless you've taken up a position inside a circle of infuriated prostitutes, but the situation was close to getting out of control. If one of those prostitutes was serious enough about protecting her turf that she would have pulled a gun, there would have been big trouble.

"What is wrong with you all?!?" I yelled. "You're acting like a bunch of kids!"

The young girl, either despite being terrified or because she was terrified, wasn't backing down. She pulled out a box cutter and flashed the blade. The others responded by whipping out blades and canisters of mace and pepper spray. One flashed a rubber-pellet gun.

I spun around in a circle to address everyone. "Would you all calm down?" I kept repeating.

My request failed. The woman with the rubber-pellet gun shot the blonde, who retaliated with a swift swipe of her box cutter.

Her blade made contact—with me. I started bleeding from my left side.

That prompted one of the prostitutes to come to my defense. "We're gonna kill her now!" she declared. (I know pastors are respected in Brazil, but still, there was something about a weapon-toting prostitute defending me that I've never quite figured out.)

All attention focused on me and my bleeding until two police cars turned the corner. I guess everyone abruptly lost their concern for me because all the prostitutes, but the young blonde, fled the scene.

"I am very sorry," she said to me. "I didn't mean to cut you."

"Put the box cutter away, please," I said. I didn't want the police to see her carrying a blade and have a reason to stop and ask questions.

After the police cars drove past us, I told her, "Listen, there are rules on the street. You shouldn't be here without permission."

She was on the verge of tears again.

Some of our team members were close by and had witnessed the incident. I motioned that I was fine. As I applied pressure to the wound, I asked the young girl for her story.

"I moved from the north of Brazil with a suitcase and about seven dollars eight months ago to look for a good job—but not as a prostitute. For the last five days, I have hardly eaten, so I decided to work the streets. Last night I got paid a hundred dollars to have sex. That's more money than I could make in a month in the north."

"You see that woman over there?" I said, pointing to the former prostitute on our team who was talking to a working prostitute. "That lady used to work the streets, but then she met Jesus Christ, who changed her life."

I began to share the story of Jesus, and the blonde listened intently.

A team member came over to check on me and noticed the blood on my shirt. "Get the police!" he yelled. "He's been cut!"

"No, no, no," I quickly responded. "Just get the first-aid kit."

He started cleaning my wound. Two female members of our team came over and began talking with the girl. My wound wasn't big at all—about an inch long—and after we bandaged it, I joined the conversation between the girl and the team members.

That night was her last as a prostitute because just a few steps from where she had slashed me, we prayed with her, and she accepted Christ as her Savior!

We gave her a ride to where she was staying and helped her get involved in a church. We were able to stay in contact with her for a year and watched her faith grow, and then she moved back to the north, a new creation in Christ.

Challenged to Demonstrate Love

Like the young blonde, numerous prostitutes came to know Christ through our Care Night. At first, our team members walked up to the prostitutes at the patio bars and engaged them in conversation. But one night, a bar owner let me have it. "I've had enough of you, Jesus freaks!" he shouted at me. "I have legal rights to have my business here, and the prostitutes help my business! If you continue to come here, I will report you to the authorities!"

So, basically, our good business had been bad for his business.

We had to come up with a new strategy and developed a "bait" approach. A male on the team would walk into a bar, look around the place, and slowly walk back outside and stand on the sidewalk. That usually drew a prostitute outside the patio barriers, and then a pair of our team members approached and began talking to her.

One evening while we were baiting, my bad knees were killing me after standing all night. I walked over to a bench, took a seat, and began praying for the ministry our team members were doing in front of me.

As I was praying, a woman who looked like a college student sat next to me.

"Are you dating tonight?" she asked in Portuguese.

I didn't understand what she meant by the question. She repeated it again. I called out to Lia, a bilingual member of our team. I told Lia in English that the woman next to me was asking me a question I couldn't understand. I repeated for her what the woman was saying.

Lia just looked at me for a couple of seconds.

"This girl is a prostitute," she informed me.

That was all the translation I needed. I asked Lia if the team was ready to leave.

Lia just looked at me again. In English, she said, "Pastor, focus. This girl beside you needs to hear about Jesus."

Appropriately rebuked, I began to talk with the young woman.

"Do you date her?" she asked in Portuguese, nodding at Lia.

"Oh, no," I said. "She is a friend of mine."

"I forgot to present myself," she said, "My name is Maria."

"My name is Eric."

"Are you just on vacation or visiting?"

"No, I live here."

"Well, what do you do?"

"I am in the life insurance business," I answered.

"That sounds interesting," she said. "Do you like it?"

"I love it. I really love it. And what do you do?"

Maria didn't reply right away, looking down to the sidewalk before answering my question.

"A month ago, I was an accountant, and it was helping me pay for my college," she said, still too ashamed to make eye contact with me. "When I lost my job, I turned to the streets to make money. I don't know what else to do."

That was not the story I expected.

"Let me understand this," I said. "You were an accountant until you got laid off, and you have no way to make money, so you came out here? Is this your first time on the streets?"

"Yes. You would be my first customer."

I didn't say anything.

Maria put her hand on my thigh, and I promptly removed it.

"I'm sorry," she said. "I'm just trying to be friendly."

That seemed like a good point in the conversation to transition to spiritual matters and begin sharing the gospel. But the Holy Spirit led me in a different direction.

"Do you think, as an accountant, you could get another job other than working the streets?"

She looked at me, a little confused.

"I don't want to offend you," she said, "but are you gay?"

I laughed.

"No, it's cool," she quickly added. "Some of my best friends are gay."

"No, I'm not gay," I told her, still chuckling.

I pointed to Lia. "Do you see that lady—the friend of mine—over there?"

Maria nodded.

"She used to be in the same situation as you are tonight, but someone came out here one night and shared the love of God with her. She accepted that love, and God changed her life."

"I don't understand," Maria said.

"Let me tell you what life insurance I'm talking about. You can have the assurance of going to heaven after you die."

Maria interrupted me. "I have a four-year-old son I need to provide for, and I have rent to pay. I went to a church yesterday and asked if they could help me pay my electricity bill so that it wouldn't be cut off, but they only offered to pray for me. The problem with the church is that they talk about love but practice very little."

I hurt hearing her disappointment in the church.

"When I sat down on this bench," I told her, "I prayed for someone to come and accept Jesus Christ. Will you make me a promise? If I'll pay for your light bill, will you come to a church service with us Sunday?"

Maria looked at me as she weighed my offer in her mind.

"My bill is fifty dollars," she said.

My next thought that came to mind was, *what church congregation couldn't afford fifty dollars?* Even a poor church could help with that amount.

I motioned for Lia to join us.

"Lia, you will not believe this, but this is the first night this girl is on the streets. She has not had a date all night, and she sat down on this bench next to me, hoping to get her first customer. She came to the right place at the right time. Can I get an 'Amen?'"

Tears appeared on Lia's face, and she bent over and hugged Maria.

Maria promised she would go to church on Sunday in a local *favela*, and we left with the hope that we would see her again Sunday. I had a feeling we would because we told her we would give her the money for her electric bill at church.

I was scheduled to speak at the service we had invited Maria to, and I was so thankful to see her enter the church on Sunday morning.

At the conclusion of my sermon, I gave an invitation for anyone wanting to accept Christ's salvation.

Maria rose from her seat and came forward.

After the service, I shared with the pastor about Maria's electricity being cut off, and he said the congregation would cover what she owed.

Because of the love that church showed Maria through finances, she became a dedicated member of the church and wound up landing another accounting job. Even after resuming her well-paying career, she continued to attend the church in the *favela* and became the church's youth director.

When people asked why she remained at that church in the slums, she would answer, "At the time of my deepest despair, this church sacrificially gave and ministered to me so that I would not seek the devil to earn money."

The Greatest of These

Ministering in Rio taught me more than ever before to see the face of Jesus in the face of every person I meet.

Taylor Hutcherson was a young lady in our church in Georgia who played the role of Jade in the movie *Courageous*. Jade was the black teenager who dated the young man caught up among drug dealers. Taylor, who had a tremendous heart for the Lord, spent a couple of months ministering with us in Rio. After a Care Night, when we had sat among the transvestites and prostitutes and talked with them, she said to me, "You know what? Sometimes, we in America say, 'We love sinners,' but we are hard-pressed to show it to people who really are down and out."

Not surprisingly, with that attitude, Taylor got involved in a night ministry in Atlanta, working with the same type of broken people she met in Rio.

That was a brilliant observation from such a young lady.

When we ministered to the unlovely, we sometimes learned more about ourselves than about them.

For those reluctant to minister to the unlovely, is it because they don't want to be perceived as accepting the lifestyle of a prostitute or a transvestite, or is it more an issue of their being uncomfortable? More than we would like to admit, it's the latter.

It was easy to go out into the streets thinking that we had something to give to the people we ministered to, but really what happened when we got there was the Holy Spirit highlighted something within us that we couldn't give and was preventing us from ministering as we should.

The truth is that we all have issues. We just try to make our issues look prettier than the unlovely's. I told the people our team ministered to during Care Nights, "Hey, I've got issues, you know that? I'm not all together! I need Jesus to help hold me together!" And when I shared emotionally like that, the looks on the faces of the transvestites and prostitutes changed. They began to cry and asked us to pray with them.

Jesus said that when we minister to the "least of these," we are ministering to Him. To be honest, in some ways, I struggle to fully understand how that works. But I do know that when we refuse to minister to the least of these in our day—the hungry, the thirsty, the sick, the transvestites, and prostitutes—it's like refusing to help Jesus Himself.

Love identifies us as Christ-followers. In John 13:34-35, Jesus said, "A new commandment I give to you, that you love one another; as I have loved you, that you also love one another. By this all will know that you are My disciples if you have love for one another" (NKJV).

Paul listed three traits in 1 Corinthians 13 that most identify us as Christians: faith, hope, and love. "But the greatest of these," he wrote, "is love." He also wrote that without love, all our religious works are nothing more than "sounding brass or a clanging cymbal." In other words, all the good things that we do are just a bunch of static noise if not accompanied by love.

That was why it was important that we demonstrated to the transvestites and prostitutes that we accepted them. We didn't have to accept what they did. We didn't, and the reason we were there was to show them that Jesus could give them a new life. In fact, as we came to know the regulars working the streets, they learned what we stood for and often "straightened up" when they saw us coming toward them. There was no doubt in their minds that we didn't care for what they did, but there was also no doubt that we did care about them.

Trust me, the hurting night people we ministered to on the streets of Rio knew the difference between Christians who truly loved and cared for them as opposed to just wanting to preach at them.

Sometimes, it requires being around unlovely people to realize how much more we need to love.

From Ramona's prayer journal:

"Lord, be a father to the fatherless (with tears and pause before continuing prayer, sensing His presence in my life throughout my own life growing up with an absent father). Protect Reese as he shares Your love on these streets. Walk with him and speak through him. In the name of Jesus, I pray. Amen."

Chapter 8

Man of Peace

Social ministries were a key component of our evangelism. We operated under the tried-and-true adage that people don't care how much you know until they know how much you care.

Luke 10 contains a familiar verse in missionaries' sermons that says, "The harvest truly is great, but the laborers are few" (NKJV). Jesus said those words as He was sending seventy disciples, in groups of twos, into parts of Judea to which He would soon be traveling. In verses 5 and 6, as part of His instructions, Jesus told the seventy that whatever houses they entered, "first say, 'Peace to this house. And if a son of peace is there, your peace will rest on it; if not, it will return to you.'"

"Peace to you" was a common greeting in those times. From that passage, I created a concept for our ministry: I wanted to be a man of peace. I did not walk into homes and communities saying, "Peace to you," but I wanted the residents and communities to see me as a man of peace—as a bringer of peace, if you will.

My priority was gaining trust. When I entered a community, I wanted residents to say, "We know that man, and we trust that man."

We had to overcome skepticism in the slums, particularly regarding money. In our early days in Rio, we had to convince people that we weren't there to take money from them, because of preachers who had previously brought prosperity theology, which also has been referred to as "health and wealth," "name it and claim it," and "blab it and grab it." Those false preachers had preyed on the Brazilians' illnesses and weaknesses. As a result, some in the slums expected hearing the gospel message to be followed by a plea for money.

I went into communities to preach for the first time, and people would call in the drug lords or paramilitary officials to speak with me.

"What do you want from these people?" they would ask me.

"Nothing," I'd say. "All we want is for their souls to be saved."

They were surprised I would come into their communities and not ask for a dime.

Although my ultimate purpose was to bring souls to Christ, to do so, I sometimes had to first prove myself as a man of peace. That applied to individuals and community leadership.

Fernando was a transvestite who worked the streets as "Fernanda." As members of our ministry team typically did, I built a rapport with Fernando through the nights we ministered on the streets. Fernando and I shared a birthday, and I felt led by God to give

Fernando a birthday card with a handwritten note. A co-worker and I handed the card to Fernando, and I asked the co-worker to read it to him in his native Portuguese.

My note expressed how I believed God had honored me through Fernando's respect of the ministry God had called me to do and told Fernando I appreciated that respect. I then continued a theme I had talked about with Fernando on the streets: God loves us, wants to change our lives, and that was what I had been praying for Fernando's life.

Fernando sat down and cried as the card was being read, right there in front of us and all the other transvestites curiously looking at him. I walked over to Fernando and reminded him, "God has a plan for your life."

Fernando told me that his mother, whom he loved dearly, had never written a letter to him like mine. When I had been impressed to write that note in the card, it seemed like a good idea, but I had no idea how God had planned to use that simple gesture to impact Fernando.

I also gave Fernando a cupcake for his birthday, by the way. That idea turned out to be a mistake because all the other transvestites wanted a cupcake, too, and I had brought only the one for Fernando's birthday. Another lesson learned on the streets of Rio.

Well beyond Fernando's birthday, we were out ministering on a rough night. It was rainy and dreary, and the weather was hurting the transvestites' business. In fact, business was so bad that the transvestites were almost in an uproar. Still, we set out to minister to them.

One transvestite didn't like what we were doing and let me know in no uncertain terms.

That's when Fernando stepped in.

"Hey, hey, hey!" he interrupted the other transvestite. "This man comes out here quite calmly, he's never asked for anything, and he comes and prays for us."

One of the other transvestites chimed in. "Yeah, he gave me this book!"

Then the transvestite turned to me with the "book" in hand. "Remember giving me this?"

It was a tract I had handed out soon after arriving in Rio—ten years earlier.

Some people in Rio kept a religious object like a tract with them for years because they believed the object's presence provided a means through which God could protect them. We couldn't do much about that belief other than pray they would read the tracts and come to know the true protection God offered them.

Because Fernando had stood up for me, everything quickly calmed down, and we were able to continue sharing the gospel.

That night, one transvestite said to me, "I don't like this life anymore. I can't stand what I'm doing. I'm taking drugs. I'm taking hormone pills, and I don't want this life anymore. Can you please help me?"

The doors had opened for us to help that transvestite because Fernando had spoken up for me, and that had come because of me writing him a card of appreciation for his birthday. Wanting to be a man of peace, I had earned Fernando's trust.

Meeting Needs

Striving to be a man of peace, though, also opened me up for criticism.

For instance, when I ministered to groups of transvestites, I never referred to any of them as "he." Instead, I made sure to say "she." I had my theology questioned because of that, but if I called a transvestite "he," I would be shut off before I could even begin sharing the gospel. Yes, I was aware that "she" was a "he," but I figured if I said "she," the gospel would prove to be the great equalizer when I was able to share it.

As you can imagine, with ministering to people in the sex industry, I heard all kinds of salty language. I would prefer never to hear some of those terms again for as long as I live, but until the transvestites and the prostitutes knew that I cared about them despite the parts of their lifestyles I did not agree with, they wouldn't care to hear what I knew about the gospel.

A well-known preacher once went out with us to minister and disagreed with my methods of evangelism. He accused me of softening the gospel. You don't have to spend much time with me to realize that I don't soften anything, much less the gospel that saved me and transformed my life.

"I will not water down the gospel and sell out to try and deceive people," the preacher declared to me.

I was taken aback. The dude had been in the country for two days and already was criticizing our team's methods of ministry.

"Instead of going out there and letting the prostitute talk to you," he chastised me, "you should go out there and quickly say, 'I'm a missionary, I'm here to share the Gospel of Truth, and I don't want to hear anything you've got to say.'"

"Would you like to try that?" I asked.

"Yes, I would," he answered.

At our next stop, I stayed in the van and sent the pastor out with an interpreter.

Needless to say, his method didn't work. He got shut down so fast that I didn't give him a second chance with another prostitute. We faced enough battles trying to earn trust on the streets, and we didn't need a preacher with a self-righteous attitude making things more difficult.

I even had someone tell me that because I put such an emphasis on reaching out to the sex-industry workers, I must have had some kind of sexual difficulty in my life. Man, that was crazy! I just saw people who needed Jesus, and I was going to be a man of peace who showed them the way to Jesus.

I don't want to come across as condemning because that's not my purpose. Instead, I want to make the point that we can't cookie-cutter ministry. Not everything that makes for successful ministry in the United States worked in Rio de Janeiro and vice-versa. When I went back to the States, I didn't say, "This is the way we do it in Rio, and this is the way you should do it here."

What does work in ministry, regardless of where you are, is grasping Christ's compassion for hurting people and following the lead of the Holy Spirit on how He wants the gospel presented to them.

Social ministry opened countless doors for us into communities. The residents of *favelas* had so many unmet needs, so we tried to help meet them.

One of the most successful social ministries we offered was basic hygiene and medical clinics. We set up our clinic equipment, and I embarked on my "advertising" routine of driving throughout the community with speakers in the back of my truck broadcasting music and information about what we were doing and where.

The residents came in large numbers, and we checked blood pressure and glucose levels, showed children how to brush their teeth, handed out cups of cold water, and gave haircuts. We provide all those free. A free haircut might not sound like much, but the two or three bucks that did not have to spend on a haircut meant a great deal to people struggling to make ends meet. Through those clinics, people responded to the gospel and trusted in Christ, and we connected them to local churches where they could grow in their faith.

I should add that part of our strategy was to build our ministry around Brazilian national teams—pastors, members of churches, teenagers. Americans came in to join us, especially college and seminary students during the summer, but we rarely brought in full American teams to work with us. That in no way is a negative reflection on American missions efforts, and we had great American volunteers come work with us. But I believed God had equipped the Brazilians with everything they needed, and I considered it important for Brazilians to minister to Brazilians. I didn't want the Brazilians to become completely reliant on Americans for ministry.

We kept at least eight people on our ministry team and experienced minimal turnover. I told our team members, "Don't bring your problem to me without also coming with a suggestion for a solution." I wanted them to think and problem-solve. I reminded them that there would be a day when we were no longer there because God at any moment could inform us it was time to head back to the United States to minister, send us to another area in Brazil, or even to another country.

To that end, my aim with the nationals on our team was to train Brazilians to take care of their own people. The Brazilians needed to see not only that God wanted to use them in their homeland but also that He had provided them what they need to take care of each other's needs.

Out of the Ashes

Any fire in a *favela* could be a huge disaster. The way the tightly packed homes climbed a mountainside only fueled a fire's path up the mountain. The shacks and many of the homes were made of wood, and even the concrete or brick homes had plenty of wooden parts. Because there was practically no space between homes, a fire could roar out of control.

Streets in the slums were usually narrow and winding, making most too difficult for fire trucks and emergency vehicles to maneuver. The best way to fight a fire was by helicopters and planes dropping water and sand onto the fire.

Reports of a fire in a slum led to assuming the worst. And that's what I did on the Sunday morning when I received a phone call about a fire in Castle City.

I was preparing to preach when news came that a fire was raging out of control in that community, which was about a twenty-minute drive from my speaking engagement. My friend on the phone said I should come to Castle City immediately. I told him I was about to speak and couldn't leave until after the service. He insisted I needed to leave right away, but I told him I couldn't.

"Let me speak to the pastor," he said.

I handed my phone to the church's pastor.

Concern filled his face as he listened to my friend describe the situation. He clicked off the call and told me, "Go, Pastor Eric. They need you in Castle City—now. Don't worry. I will preach the service."

Ramona and the girls were with me, and we quickly departed. I didn't want them near the dangers of the fire and told them I would first take them to our house on the edge of Castle City. Before we reached our home, we could see tar-black smoke rolling into the sky above the community.

We lived on the outskirts of Castle City when we first started working in Rio and still knew many of the people there. After I dropped my family off, the smoke showed no signs of the fire diminishing. The smell grew thicker. I dreaded what I might see when I arrived.

Police had blocked off the street at the bottom of the hill. I told the policemen standing guard that I was a pastor and had come to help the people. They allowed me through the blockade, but only on foot.

Flames were finishing off some buildings and leaping out of the windows of others. In apartments yet to be swallowed by fire, residents were throwing their possessions through their windows. The narrow streets were catching their mattresses, furniture, televisions, lamps, clothes, and whatever else they hoped to save.

People were running around in all directions and screaming for help. The helicopters and small planes added to the chaos, dropping water and sand onto the buildings and people below.

It was snowing ash, and the smoke made breathing difficult.

I had to stop walking momentarily to comprehend what was taking place in front of me. All I could pray was, *God, help us!*

I was jolted from my stunned spectator mode when someone recognized me and shoved a bucket of water in my hands, pulling me into a bucket brigade of people tossing water on the fire. The task was much bigger than the human chain could handle, but the families, bless their hearts, were willing to attempt anything that offered even the smallest hope of preventing everything they owned from being destroyed.

Even while hurriedly grabbing buckets from the person behind me and passing them to the person ahead of me, I was already thinking about what would be needed after the fire burned itself out. I spotted a top paramilitary official in the community in the crowd, looking completely helpless, and hopped out of the line. I told him our ministry owned a gigantic, circus-type tent that could provide shelter for about forty families. He gladly accepted my offer and asked how many men I needed to set up the tent. I told him twenty or thirty. He instructed a soldier with him, "Go get the pastor a big truck and thirty-five men."

The commander designated a soccer field as the site for our tent, and with his men's assistance, we set that tent up in two hours. I had never seen that big tent go up so fast.

Word spread that we were setting up a tent, and people started rushing toward the soccer field before we had finished securing the tent. People yelled and argued about the limited space under the tent, and if not for the timely arrival of fifteen policemen, the scene would have soon gotten out of hand.

More than forty families squeezed into the tent, but probably more than two hundred fifty families had nowhere to go.

The fire left the area virtually unrecognizable. Burned-out shells of concrete and brick buildings lined the streets. The streets were filled with burned clothes, furniture, and other possessions. Many families lost everything they owned. The residents did not have a lot of possessions to begin with, but no matter how much or how little it is, someone's everything is everything.

Miraculously, not one person died in the fire.

We transitioned into the recovery stage and placed an appeal by radio for people throughout Rio to donate anything they could because the fire had left most of the people in Castle City with nothing.

I didn't need long to realize that the police expected me to take charge of the tent-food-clothing distribution project. I was glad to help, but it was an overwhelming assignment. The tendency in Rio was for missionaries and pastors to be expected to do everything in those kinds of situations. I had to draw lines and insist that community leaders handle logistical and administrative responsibilities, and I turned over to the paramilitary authorities the tasks of keeping order and helping distribute goods and foods. I needed to prevent becoming so bogged down with duties the paramilitary could handle that I couldn't check on the spiritual and emotional needs of those left homeless by the fire.

I prioritized scheduling Sunday morning worship services and Tuesday night Bible studies for the new tent community. Among the first things people ask in times of disaster and crisis was, "Where was God when we needed Him, and why did He allow this to happen?" It was important I answer their questions: God was where He has always been—right in their midst. Many in Castle City had nothing material left after the fire, but I was thankful for opportunities to remind them that they could always have God.

The people living under the tent were hungry for God's Word. That wasn't surprising, because people tend to be more open to God during times of pain and suffering. They also were hungry for anything that would lift their spirits. To that end, the paramilitary authorities offered to pay for a barbeque picnic for the families to celebrate that everyone had survived the fire. On multiple occasions, I made sure God received the people's thanks for emerging with no loss of life.

More than 800 families attended the celebration service and picnic. That was a lot of barbeque! The families enjoyed the celebration—and the free food—and the paramilitaries were pleased to have fed so many people. The free barbeque made them look good in the residents' eyes.

I was asked to preach at the celebration service, but I thought that privilege should belong to a local pastor because the local pastors were the true shepherds of the *favelas*. I was honored to work alongside many humble pastor-shepherds committing their lives to minister in Rio's *favelas*. They didn't make the news, and their names weren't known outside their communities, but God knew them because they were taking care of His sheep.

Pastor Nino preached a powerful message that ended with 88 people accepting Christ for the first time and 112 recommitting their lives to Him.

We didn't have only a big altar call, though. Many pastors, church leaders, and counselors were at the event and spoke with those who had professed their faith in Jesus. The new believers were given information about how to get involved in local churches. Many of them began attending Pastor Nino's church.

The celebration service was a spiritual high point for Castle City, a Romans 8:28 moment for sure: "And we know that in all things God works for the good of those who love him, who have been called according to his purpose" (NKJV).

Before the fire, many in the community had heard the gospel message but had put off responding. Life took on a different meaning in Castle City when the residents lost their possessions and realized they could have lost their lives. In a place where people lived with no guarantee of tomorrow, the fire served as a sobering reminder it was much better to get right with God while the opportunity still existed.

We still faced a monumental challenge, though, with all the families who had no place to live. Within only a few days, David Brown of Baptist Global Response (now Send Relief) supplied funds for a semi-permanent shelter. The Brazilians supplied the labor and skill, constructing a facility out of cement and wooden poles and with a solid roof to keep out the rains. The inside was divided into spaces for families, creating enough room for forty-eight more displaced families to move in.

Everyone who lived under our tent rebuilt their home, found a new place to live, moved in with relatives, or made new living arrangements.

For eleven months following the fire, I taught the Tuesday night Bible studies. More than 100 people regularly attended. From that Bible study, two new churches were birthed and set off on a path of consistent growth.

I remain grateful I was able to witness God do great things in Castle City's time of trouble. Many people found Christ or rededicated their lives to Him after the fire. An attitude of togetherness sprang out of the paramilitary authorities and the residents working toward common goals of, first, survival and, then, rebuilding. God crafted an amazing amount of good out of a desperate situation.

An interesting development further cemented my love for the people who lived in the *favelas*. Inside each *favela*, there was a sense of community that might not have been visible on good days. But on bad days, the people rallied together, and that was evident in the hours and days immediately following the fire.

We had immediately made known throughout Rio the great need in Castle City, asking for donations to help the residents. Most of the contributions we received came not from the more affluent areas of Rio, though, but from within Castle City itself.

Residents dropping off items at the tent told me, "I don't have much, but take this and give it to them." They brought buckets of food and donated their time to prepare meals for the tent families.

Eventually, we began receiving help from outside the community. But for the first couple of weeks, the residents of Castle City sustained the recovery efforts. I was so impressed that poor people who had survived the fire had dug deep to aid those among them who had lost everything.

The very people who had the least to give gave the most.

Jacarepaguá for Jesus

Our social ministries attracted the attention of government officials, and they came to us at times with opportunities we viewed as additional chances to provide ministry.

We didn't plan our ministry strategies in Rio so that we could gain the favor of politicians because everything we did was designed to gain the favor of God. But I believe that when we as believers gain God's favor, many times He then gives His people favor with the authorities. There are historical exceptions, of course, but Daniel and his three Hebrew friends come to mind as an example of that principle.

We acted honestly, wisely, and respectfully toward the civil authorities while maintaining our allegiance to Christ. God then granted us favor through the trust in us government officials displayed.

That led to the establishment of an annual day that made a significant impact in the community of Jacarepaguá.

I received a phone call one day from a representative of Rio de Janeiro's governor. The city of Rio de Janeiro is the capital of the state of Rio de Janeiro. Apparently, the governor had heard of our social ministry successes and invited me to lead a devotional for his staff at the governor's palace.

I was pumped up about the opportunity and began pondering what future opportunities might result from that one. But when I gave the devotion, I didn't think anyone was listening because many of the governor's staff were moving around the room and talking on their cell phones.

You can imagine my surprise when I received a second invitation to lead a staff devotion and, this time, to meet privately with the governor.

The second invitation cranked up the wheels in my mind. I wondered if God had a secondary purpose for my one-on-one session with the governor. I began to envision a "Jacarepaguá for Jesus" day that would be a celebration to lift Jesus' name in the community.

Jacarepaguá is the fourth-largest neighborhood, size-wise, in the city of Rio de Janeiro. It is the ninth largest in terms of population. Jacarepaguá, in Rio's West Zone, had large open areas where music festivals, cultural events, and even car races were held. To me, it seemed like a perfect place for a celebration event. As a middle-class neighborhood surrounded by *favelas*, Jacarepaguá also offered a good representation of our ministry focus. And with the most television studios of any area in Latin America, a celebration would carry the potential of attracting substantial media coverage.

I filled in one of our team members about my pending meeting with the governor and my ideas for a parade and all-day festival devoted to Jesus. I also sought the counsel of the local pastors. When Ramona and I first arrived in Rio, we met with thirty-two local pastors and asked them seven questions. The last was an important one we had saved for the end: "What can we do for you and your church as missionaries?" We were blown away and saddened when the pastors—including one who had been pastoring there for forty-two years—told us we were the first missionaries who had come in and asked them that question. Instead, previous missionaries had moved in as American experts, already knowing what the local pastors needed to know. From my first day in Rio, I sought the pastors' advice, and they proved to be sources of godly and wise counsel.

My idea for the celebration was no different. One of the local pastors surprised me by suggesting I *not* ask the governor to sponsor the celebration.

"Instead," he recommended, "work with a few of the city commissioners and build a support base at their level instead of at the governor's level."

In my prayer time, I received confirmation of the pastor's advice, and the more I thought about it, the wiser his recommendation appeared. As chief executive of the state, the governor needed to satisfy many people. He would have had many factors to consider before approving the event. But there were fifty-one elected city commissioners and seeking and gaining the support of a few of them would carry less risk because it would not require the "official" approval of the entire state government.

I had come to know one of the city commissioners, Frank. He liked the idea and promised to seek out a cosponsor for Jacarepaguá for Jesus. Ramona, I, and the evangelism team entered a season of prayer for the celebration. We knew the resources of heaven would be required for such an event to come together.

After some time, Frank came through on his promise when he secured another commissioner's agreement to co-sponsor the event with him. They took the idea to the full council, and forty-nine of the fifty-one members voted to approve our event.

The first Jacarepaguá for Jesus was scheduled for September 6, 2005, and it was set up to become an annual event. Our team was so excited that the special day had been granted that we could do no more than cry and sing praises to God. Gaining approval was a major answer to prayer that could come only from God.

My second turn for a devotional at the governor's palace came while we were planning the event. Interest and momentum in our day were building, causing the governor's staff to be more attentive this time. There were no cell phone calls or disinterested people walking around the room. Everyone placed full attention on my words.

I spoke to the staff about the basic message of love. "If we would understand that God loves us and understand that we need to love others," I told them, "this city would change. You are leaders, so it is my prayer that when you go to work, you would not think of your own interests, but the interests of the people."

I then met with the governor, who told me he was a Christian and asked if I would pray for him and his staff. As long as he was governor, he said, he wanted us to stay in touch. When the governor voiced his support for the parade and festival in Jacarepaguá, I became excited at the thought of state support potentially leading to day-for-Jesus events in other communities.

Frank was not a Christian, but his wife was. She was chief of staff in her husband's office, and she was a mover and shaker when it came to planning for Jacarepaguá for Jesus. Eager to help spread the word about the first event, she invited me to Frank's office to communicate the vision for the day with his staff. I shared how I wanted September 6 to be a day for Christ to be lifted up and for people to have the opportunity to put their faith in Him. I wanted it to be a day to put aside the violence and lawlessness too common in the city's poorer communities.

On another day, Frank took me to the backside of Jacarepaguá, to where the poorest of the poor in the slum lived. The area was filled with wooden shacks connected by muddy paths. A few chickens darted here and there while children played on a makeshift soccer field.

"We don't have a church back here to share the message of Jesus Christ," Frank told me in a sad tone. Now, however, there is a church in that spot that God provided for the community, and it's a church that faithfully shares the gospel.

As September neared, we took our medical clinics into the area on Saturdays to teach the poor kids how to brush their teeth, to give them free haircuts; and to check glucose and blood pressure levels for the adults. Because we were there to meet needs and asked for nothing in return, trust in us was beginning to build as word of the event was beginning to spread.

Radio and television stations interviewed me in the days leading up to the event, and when journalists asked six randomly selected citizens their opinions about having a special day for evangelism, five voiced their approval. One said it was "painfully evident that Rio de Janeiro needs Somebody to look to." Another commented that the people of Jacarepaguá needed a divine revelation on how to treat one another.

The community needed a day like Jacarepaguá for Jesus.

We expected 100 people might show up for the parade. We slightly missed our estimate because when the big day arrived, an estimated 1,500 people marched through the streets of Jacarepaguá. The gospel was proclaimed throughout the day. We had a Christian concert. We had special speakers. We distributed food to the poor.

Support for the special day included the attendance of twenty-five pastors and hundreds of members from thirteen churches from three denominations. We were thrilled to see a significant turnout from young people. All ages were well represented.

Media broadcast and wrote about the event statewide, bringing added credibility for us among politicians and the entire state. Most important, God received the glory for that day and for every Jacarepaguá for Jesus celebration that took take place in the years that followed.

A personal highlight of the first event was marching in the parade alongside so many different pastors and believers from so many different churches. Despite some theological or practical differences, we agreed on one thing: Jesus is Lord over all!

Christians should take advantage of every opportunity to gather and display love and unity because the world notices when followers of Jesus are unified and love one another.

It's true that people don't care how much we know until they know how much we care. Sometimes, the first step is for us Christians to show how much we care for each other.

From Ramona's prayer journal:
"Lord, teach me to love my husband and children more. Teach us to love the *Cariocas* in practical ways. May we give out of the overflow."

Chapter 9

Truthfully Speaking...

Would you lie to save your life? Or to save someone else's? To take the issue a step further, is withholding information the equivalent of lying?

Ramona and I had to face those questions before we left for the mission field. Then again, after we arrived in Brazil.

During training at the IMB missionary learning center, we were taught not to lie in dangerous or life-or-death situations. But we also were taught to keep our mouths shut in certain instances—to not say more than we were required to say. Fortunately, I had picked up experience in that area growing up in tough neighborhoods.

It's one thing to say, "I won't lie to save my life" at the training center in Virginia. It's quite another to live that out on the streets of Rio's *favelas*.

Ramona and I determined before going to the field that we wanted to honor God as missionaries, and as part of that, we wouldn't lie about anything, even if our lives were endangered. God desires that we be truthful and honest people.

But still, those are intriguing questions I posed. As I considered them for myself, I opened my Bible to see what guidance Scripture provided.

It's easy to find biblical heroes who lied.

Abraham lied when he said his wife, Sarah, was his sister (Genesis 20). Isaac, Abraham's son, told the same lie regarding his wife, Rebekah (Genesis 26). Like father, like son, I guess. King David, described in Scripture as a man after God's own heart, lived a lie after impregnating Bathsheba and then arranging to have her husband, Uriah, killed in battle to cover it up (2 Samuel 11).In the New Testament, three of the four Gospel writers told us that Peter lied three times about knowing Jesus (Matthew 26, John 14, Luke 22, John 18).

In none of those cases, though, was lying commended. While Abraham, Isaac, David, and Peter are biblical examples of heroes who lied, they are not biblical examples that it is *permissible* to lie.

In one case in the Bible, a person's lying ended with a positive result. Rahab, a prostitute in Jericho, lied to save the lives of the Israelites, spying in the city before Joshua's army attacked (Joshua 2, 6). Rahab's actions in hiding and saving the spies were commended in the New Testament (Hebrews 11:31, James 2:25). She also was an ancestor of Jesus Christ (Matthew 1:5).

Perhaps we should view Rahab as the exception that proves the rule—that God can work through flawed human beings to accomplish His will. The end result does not mean that Rahab was right to lie. She was a pagan woman who did not know the character of God and was doing what she thought at the time was right. Who knows if she would have lied if she had possessed a different spiritual status at that stage in her life.

The biblical principle for communication among Christians in the body of Christ is clear. Paul condemned lying in relationships when he wrote in Ephesians 4:25, "Therefore, putting away lying, 'Let each one of you speak truth with his neighbor,' for we are members of one another" (NKJV).

Having said all that, I'll ask again: Would you lie to save your life? Or to save someone else's? Is withholding information the equivalent of lying?

Under Interrogation

Pastors know church growth can present problems. Most of the time, a pastor loves those problems because of what they represent. If a church needs a new building because its attendance has grown so much that its current facility no longer is adequate, that's a problem—a good problem.

We had some "church growth," if you will, that presented a problem for me. A Bible study I was leading in Canal Vale had outgrown the house where we met. With nowhere else to put the people, one week, our group moved into the small street, more like an alleyway, outside the house.

During our meeting, around 5:30 p.m., as I was teaching on Rahab, the prostitute, we heard gunfire. That's not exactly breaking news in a *favela*. The gunshots didn't sound too close—no one ducked when we heard them—and we continued right on ahead with our study. Just another evening in the *favelas*!

Suddenly, a young man sprinted past our group. He was carrying a clear bag with what looked like marijuana and crack cocaine in one hand and a 9mm pistol in the other. Again, not exactly huge news in that area, but worth at least a small headline. We paused to watch him run out of sight.

As we resumed our study, a policeman came running toward us from the same direction the young man had come. Now that was breaking news because I couldn't recall seeing a policeman pursuing anyone on foot in the *favelas*.

"Which way did he go?!?" he shouted to us, stopping to hopefully receive a quick answer.

The reasons the questions I posed in this chapter are difficult ones because every situation is unique. That's why it is important to have principles to live by—such as "I won't lie"—and then trust the Holy Spirit for the wisdom to know the right thing to say and do when those unique situations arise.

"Who?" I asked as I looked down at my Bible.

"That young guy who just came through here!" the policeman

answered through heavy breathing.

No one in our group said a word—every one of them, plus the policeman, looked straight at me.

In that short amount of time, I thought about Rahab's story. Considering the man was on a mad dash with a bag of drugs and a gun, I felt confident he wasn't one of God's spies.

"I'm not sure," I blurted out.

Without the answer he was looking for, the policeman resumed his chase down the street. After watching the policeman take off, I looked back at our group. If their eyes had been laser pointers, I would have had been blinded by the red beams because every eye in the group was zeroed in on my eyes.

A chicken in the coop only seconds from having his neck wrung would have felt less cornered than I did—and by my own people at that.

I shrugged. "What are you looking at me for?" I was confused, and my Bible study members knew it. My lack of confidence in the situation was on display for all to see.

One member answered. "Because you were leading the Bible study, and the policeman was asking you!"

The more I stood in front of the group and thought about my response to the policeman, the worse I began to feel about not being straightforward. I hadn't told a lie, but I also hadn't told the policeman everything I knew. I felt like a hypocrite and unworthy of continuing to teach the group from the Bible. Filled with guilt, my next step was to ask God for forgiveness. I looked toward heaven to do so. In my line of sight between me and heaven, on a rooftop across the street, stood three armed men staring down at me.

A chill came over me when I realized that if I had been observed pointing the policeman in the direction the young man had fled, those shooters likely would have taken me out on the spot. And, perhaps, some of the Bible study members, too, as a reminder of what happens when someone snitches in the *favelas*.

God protected me, for sure, and probably all of us without us knowing the potential danger on the roof. I'm not smart enough to develop that into a theological case study, but that's what happened.

After the Bible study, one of the men from the rooftop walked across the street and up to me.

"You did well, Pastor," he said. "Thank you."

I looked into his eyes to answer. "When I was allowed into this community to share the gospel, I was instructed that I do not see anything or hear anything. All that I am to know is that Jesus saves."

I hadn't shaken off the effects of the evening when I stepped into my truck and started toward home. The phone call early during my trip didn't help any.

"Think well," the unidentifiable voice said when I answered.

That was the complete message. "Think well." I couldn't help but wonder whether it was a warning from someone connected with the rooftop shooters.

Minutes later, my phone rang again. The police asked me to report to their station immediately.

"Why?" I asked.

"It can't be discussed over the phone," I was told. "But you need to come now. We do not want to make an appearance at your house."

I didn't want them to make an appearance at my house, either. I called Ramona, filled her in, expressed my concerns over a situation quickly deteriorating, and asked her to pray for me.

It was about 7 p.m. when I arrived at the police station, and a long day immediately got longer. I was ushered into a room with a desk and a chair, pointed to sit in the chair, and promptly accused of drug trafficking. My bald head was profusely sweating, and only partly because the station had no air conditioning.

Two policemen built their case against me by telling me things such as "Your truck looks like a police vehicle" and "You have easy access into that community."

I went into my military mode—if captured, provide only name, rank, and serial number.

"Sir, I am an American missionary. I was appointed in 1999 in Sacramento, California, by the Southern Baptist Convention. I made a commitment to the Lord that I would preach Jesus everywhere I go. I can assure you that I am involved in no conspiracy or any trafficking and that the only thing I do is preach that Jesus saves."

The policemen grew agitated with me responding to every question or accusation in that manner.

One of them pulled out a photo. It was taken in Canal Vale, and I was standing by my truck talking with a well-known person in the community. (Remember what I said earlier about being "known" in a community?)

"Then tell me," the policeman asked, "why were you talking to this fellow at 2 a.m.?"

"I am an American missionary. I was appointed in 1999 in Sacramento, California, by the Southern Baptist Convention. The only thing I do is preach, at whatever hour, that Jesus saves. I can assure you that I am not involved in any conspiracy or any trafficking."

The other officer walked around and sat on the table right in front of me. My hand was resting on the table, and he sat squarely on my hand, making sure his pistol dug into my knuckles.

"You did not answer the question," he forcefully said, standing so close to me that splatters of spit hit my face. "This picture shows that you were talking to this fellow at 2 a.m. Why were you there?"

I replied with my pat answer.

That brought the second-in-command into the questioning. Furious, he leaned down, so we were face-to-face. "I am tired of your baloney. We need to get down to the truth, and you better answer our questions because you are about to be charged and possibly expelled from this country."

When he said that, I recalled being instructed in missionary training that if captured or detained by a government, we should provide the authorities with a toll-free number to call to reach people at the missions agency who would verify my missionary status.

"Sir, you can call Jim Sessions at this phone number, and he can confirm to you that I am an American missionary and that I was appointed in 1999 in Sacramento, California, by the Southern Baptist Convention. He can also assure you that I am here only to preach the gospel and that if he needs to contact a lawyer to represent me, he will do that. I will not respond to any more questions concerning your threats made at me."

I felt fairly confident that answer would cause my interrogators to reconsider continuing with their line of questioning. It turned out I was overconfident.

"We don't give a flip who Jim Sessions is," one said. "We also don't think you're a pastor. What type of pastor would be up at 2 a.m. in Canal Vale?"

Each time they asked a question, I responded with my stock answer.

I changed my answer, though, for one question from the second-in-command.

"Have you ever been in the military?"

"Yes, sir."

The three policemen looked at each other and said in unison, *"Faz sentido!"* ("That figures.") Then they stormed out of the room.

I remained alone in the interrogation room for forty-five minutes. I sat there praying and wondering what would happen next. It was nearing 10 p.m.—I had been in the room for three hours—when one of the officers returned.

"You're free to go," he said. "We are not going to charge you with anything. But we do not want to see you ever again in that community at 2 a.m."

"I am an American missionary," I replied. "I was appointed—"

"Yeah, yeah. I get it," the officer said, cutting me off. "Appointed in 1999 in Sacramento, California, by the Southern Baptist Convention," he continued in a mocking tone. "We've already heard that. Just stop. Just stop."

"But seriously," I told him, "if you ever see me in this community again, it's because I am there to preach—"

"Yeah, I know. Blah, blah, blah, preaching about Jesus."

Then he escorted me out of the station.

I met with the two officers again only three days later when we held another Bible study in Canal Vale. I didn't want my truck seen in that community, so I took a motorcycle taxi to and from the Bible study. On the way out of Canal Vale, we passed the two cops in a police car going the opposite direction. They whipped their car around, pulled our motorcycle over, and immediately ordered the driver and me up against a wall with our hands raised.

They searched us, and the most significant items they found on me were my Bible with my Bible study notes inside.

"Officer," I began, "I am an American missionary, and I just had a Bible study—"

The officer interrupted. "You forgot about the convention and everything else."

"No, I didn't," I replied. "You didn't give me a chance to finish."

Everyone laughed, except for the confused motorcycle driver, and then we were on our way back out of the community.

Three days after that, I preached at a new church in that area. Three guys on motorcycles came up to me and forced me to go with them to speak to the drug lord on top of his mountain. I was questioned about why I had been observed laughing with two policemen three days earlier. (I'm telling you, there were eyes watching everything in those communities.)

I answered that I had nothing to do with the police. The drug dealers told me they knew of my visit to the police station, and I also had to explain that situation.

"But why were you talking to the officers three nights ago?" one of the men asked.

I replied that if they ever saw me talking with police, one of two things was taking place: I was being interrogated by them, or I was sharing the gospel with them.

"I am not," I emphatically stated, "working with the police in any way."

"But you were laughing with them!" the man shot back.

Whack!

Before I could begin to formulate an answer, the top guy slapped his man across the top of his head.

"Don't be a fool!" he told him. "If he had been an informer to the police, they wouldn't have stopped and ordered him up against the wall! Don't be an idiot, you idiot!

Back to the Questions

So, should a Christian lie? My answer, as I shared earlier, is no. I don't want to deliberately tell a falsehood to mislead someone. But, as my experiences proved, sometimes, in some situations, it was better to leave certain things unsaid.

Life, however, is complicated, whether you're a missionary or not. We can find ourselves caught in situations where the answer to what we should do doesn't seem so clear-cut, where the situation is unique. I am grateful that when these tests come at us—often unannounced and catching us completely off-guard—God has provided the Holy Spirit to guide us if we let Him, moment by moment.

I like to apply two other verses to this topic.

The first is Matthew 10:16, where Jesus is sending His disciples out for ministry in enemy territory. Jesus gave them an unusual piece of advice: "Behold, I send you out as sheep in the midst of wolves. Therefore be wise as serpents and harmless as doves." (NKJV)

The second is Romans 16:19, where Paul writes, "For your obedience has become known to all. Therefore I am glad on your behalf, but I want you to be wise in what is good, and simple concerning evil" (NKJV).

"Wise as serpents" has nothing to do with the type of evil demonstrated by the serpent in the Garden of Eden. It means skillful or intelligent. And "harmless as doves" means innocent. Jesus was wise and innocent in His dealings with authority, and that's what I want to be as I maintain my allegiance to God's kingdom.

From Ramona's prayer journal:

"Lord, teach us, but especially Reese and his team, to be as wise as serpents and as harmless as doves as we walk the streets of Rio ministering in your name."

Chapter 10

Fear as a Companion

I consider fear a form of worship because what we fear, we elevate in status. Think about it: if you fear a big ol' mean and ugly dog, you are going to respect and give reverence to that dog. Thus, whatever we fear, we worship.

Fear was a cloud persistently hanging over the *favelas*. Because the people were trapped there due to being poor, they had to live with the risks and fears associated with drugs and crime. The government was unable to bring about stability in the *favelas*, especially those run by the drug lords. As a result, every resident had to fend for himself.

The leaders of the communities—and along with them, the rules—could change overnight with no warning signs. Sometimes, the only way for a resident of a *favela* to learn the rules had changed was to unknowingly break one. Because the police held little control, justice often played out in vigilante fashion—as illustrated by the story about Gary.

However, the people seemed content with that type of justice system. The residents often aligned their allegiance to whoever could keep order and institute a system of rules in their community. Yet within that system, fear ruled. The people lived in outright fear of violating the authorities' rules. And that provided a challenge in sharing the gospel.

Ramona and I went to Rio with a message of grace, mercy, and forgiveness and we found ourselves in an environment in which most of the people had not experienced grace, mercy, *or* forgiveness. Even when those who lived in the slums did receive God's forgiveness, they still had to live under the heels of authorities. A part of me understood why some there questioned what practical benefit there was to accepting Christ.

I speak in three volume levels. In addition to my normal conversation level, I tend to speak softly when I am reflective. And when I get worked up, I get loud. If you want to hear my loud voice, tell me, "But Brother Eric, you just need to tell the people that the Bible says, 'there is no fear in love,' and that 'perfect love casts out fear.'"

The message, stated in that manner, would not preach in the slums of Rio.

We need to consider the full context of that passage, 1 John 4:17-19: *"Love has been perfected among us in this: that we may have boldness in the day of judgment; because as He is, so are we in this world. There is no fear in love; but perfect love casts out fear because fear involves torment. But he who fears has not been made perfect in love. We love Him because He first loved us"* (NKJV).

I promise that the people we ministered to saw more torment than they did the type of love described there.

So that was why I needed at the same time to show them as much of God's love as we could. I also needed to model how to deal with fear.

Preacher's Helper

Two of my greatest fears in life are being shot and contracting a life-threatening disease. Naturally, ministering in the slums of Rio brought me more opportunities than I preferred to deal with those two fears. Included was the first funeral I preached in Brazil, which I thought at the time might turn out to be my last.

I had first met Frank, who helped make Jacarepaguá for Jesus a reality before he had been elected a city commissioner. At the time, Frank was president of a neighborhood government association. While we were in his community one morning to preach the gospel and show the *JESUS* film, he walked over to introduce himself.

Frank welcomed our team and offered to let us set up our film projector and loudspeakers in the main plaza in front of the neighborhood association building.

The prime location attracted about 300 people into the plaza and many more across the street. At the end of the film, hundreds of people came forward for prayer. Frank's wife was among them. I prayed with her, and although she didn't accept Christ that day, she definitely opened her heart to God and later became a Christian.

Our family became friends with Frank and his wife. As an example of how careful I had to be to remain neutral in politics, I declined when Frank asked me to support his campaign to become a city commissioner. I told Frank I couldn't be involved in political campaigns but that I could pray for him, and especially that he would become a believer and accomplish God's will for his life.

Frank needed three tries to win an election, but he became a commissioner in a paramilitary-controlled community. When his wife later told me that she had become a Christian, I was briefly speechless—that doesn't happen to me often—and then encouraged her to pray for her husband and that he would serve his community with integrity. She did, and she also became outspoken within the community about her faith.

Because of the relationship we had built up with Frank, he called one day to ask if I would conduct the funeral of a leading paramilitary commander who had been killed the night before by a drug gang from another community. Frank also asked me to claim the body from the morgue and handle the arrangements for the funeral and burial.

At the morgue, I was stunned by the number of bodies crammed side by side into the room. The odor of the decomposing bodies almost knocked me over, and I had to step outside for fresh air before I could continue.

The commander had been shot in the head, and although his family had provided a picture of him, I was concerned I would not be able to recognize him. I didn't want to think about what it would be like for the family if I picked out the wrong body. It took a while, but the morgue attendant and I were able to match a body to the picture. I left the morgue—not soon enough, as far as I was concerned—to go to the funeral home with papers granting authority for the body to be picked up and prepared for burial.

I went back into the paramilitary-controlled community later that day, certain I was under surveillance, and began to feel nervous about meeting with the family members in their home. I considered that the authorities could take offense with me making such a bold statement of Christian witness, but I was committed to sharing the gospel and was not going to water down the gospel no matter what.

Frank met me at the deceased commander's home and ushered me through the large crowd that had gathered outside.

I told Frank about my concerns.

"Pastor, you're in charge," was all he said.

I offered words of sympathy and sorrow for the loss to the family in the room where they had gathered. Then I told them the Bible says in Hebrews 9:27 that man is appointed to die once and then be judged. "We are all going to die someday," I said. "A man is born crying, and then there will be a day when we cry because that man has died. The Bible says that we can die with God or without God."

Pausing, I took note of how intently the family was listening. I wasn't sure if it was because the Lord was at work in their hearts or because they were trying to understand my broken Portuguese. Regardless, when no one made a sound, I continued.

"The first reason I am here is that I love people. The second reason I am here is that God called me to Brazil to share the gospel. The third reason is that God called me to speak on behalf of the King of kings' love for you. Jesus said, 'Greater love has no man than this, than to lay down one's his life for his friends.'[i]

"Imagine I am in a room with one other person, and someone walks in with a gun. The guy with the gun says, 'I have to shoot one of you.' Then my friend says to the guy with the gun, 'Shoot me. Don't shoot Eric.' That is like God's love for us. Even while we didn't care to know about His love, He still came and died for us.[ii]

"This man left this life while we are still here. If he could say something to you, I am almost sure he would say, 'Love God and give your life to God.'"

I did not believe the murdered man to be a Christian. I imagined him to be like the rich nonbeliever in Luke 16 who, after dying and entering the afterlife, wanted to get a message to his family encouraging them to repent of their sins.

"I want to give you a picture of what God did for you. He sent Jesus to die on the cross." I stretched out my arms to illustrate. "And they drove nails through Jesus' hands and feet. The Bible says on that day of Jesus' crucifixion that there were two thieves on crosses, one to His left and one to His right. One of them went to heaven and the other to hell. Why did one crook go to heaven and the other to hell? According to the Bible, before the crook who went to heaven died, he asked Jesus, 'When you go into Your kingdom, will You please remember me?' Jesus responded, 'This day you shall be with Me in Paradise.' But the other crook instead mocked Jesus.[iii]

"So let me share with you my understanding of this true story. One crook recognized he was a crook and in need of a Savior, so he asked Jesus to remember him. He asked Jesus to save him. On the other hand, the other crook did not recognize his need for a Savior, so he chose to reject Christ. All of us can choose whether or not we need Jesus as our Savior, just like those two thieves did two thousand years ago. We need to be saved from our sins. Let me tell you about me. I don't walk on water, and if you were ever in my truck with me driving and saw me having to fend for myself in this traffic, you wouldn't think I was a preacher. I have weaknesses that God is changing in my life. I am not completely transformed, but I am in the transforming process."

Even though this was a somber occasion, I was really into the flow of my message for the family. Apparently, I wasn't the only one because the victim's grandmother stood and came toward me. She was a thin woman standing about five feet five or so, and I had no idea what was about to happen as she turned to face the family.

"What this preacher is trying to tell you," she said in a strong voice, "is that we all need Jesus Christ as our Savior."

Then she turned back to face me and said, "Go right ahead."

"She said it best with fewer words," I continued. "I am going to pray, and if you want Jesus to come into your heart, you can repeat the prayer. If you mean it, Jesus will transform your life."

With the grandmother still next to me, I prayed and then asked that anyone who had said that prayer would raise his or her hand so I could help connect them to a church.

"Ask them to stand up!" the grandmother instructed me.

The family must have known that when Grandma speaks, she means business because eleven people immediately rose from their seats. Inside, I rejoiced at the number of changed lives.

Before I could say the people could take their seats, the grandmother took control again.

"Preacher, come pray for each of them and put your hand on their heads as you do it!"

Frank was sitting in the back of the room, and when I made eye contact with him, he gave me a look that seemed to say, *What are you waiting for? You heard the lady!*

I started praying for the people as grandma ordered, beginning with a nine-year-old boy. I couldn't help but weep as I prayed for him. I made my way around the room, praying for each of the eleven where they stood. Then I heard Frank clear his throat next to me. I assumed he was indicating that it was time for me to wrap up.

I had misread his signal, though, because he motioned that he wanted me to pray for him, too. I began praying for Frank without placing my hand on his head. Frank grabbed my hand and put it on his head. Again, I could have shouted for joy right there during the makeshift funeral service.

It's common in Brazil for a funeral service to be held at the cemetery, and when I concluded praying, Frank asked me to announce to those inside the home and to those gathered outside that the funeral would be the following morning at the cemetery.

Shootout at the Cemetery

It was my first official funeral service in Brazil and my first in Portuguese, and I arrived at the cemetery a half-hour early. The scene was nothing like what I had experienced in the States—armed paramilitary men from Castle City were stationed inside the cemetery's high stone walls.

Near the announced time for the funeral, two busloads of people arrived, followed by the hearse. I stood beside the gravesite as the hearse backed up next to me.

Suddenly, a round of shots rang out.

People began screaming and running for cover. I started a sprint toward the cemetery office. The people inside were shutting the door as I arrived and had no intention of holding it open for me. With momentum from my run, I lowered a shoulder into the door as it was closing and shouted, "I'm coming in there!" The people closing the door almost hit the floor from the force of my blow.

By the time they shut and locked the door, I had claimed my hiding spot under the desk. Three people were in the office.

"Jesus, Jesus, Jesus!" a woman in the office shouted.

"That's the name to call!" I shouted back.

She looked at me like I was crazy, but I wasn't. It was Jesus we needed at that exact moment.

"Oh, Lord Jesus," she said, looking toward me, "look what he's brought here!"

Me? I hadn't brought the gunfire to the cemetery! I was just a preacher there for a funeral—and someone else's, not mine.

The gravedigger was in the office.

"Lord, I hope I don't have to dig two or three more holes today," he said.

I stayed under the desk, lying on the floor, and praying the whole time as the gunshots continued.

The police evidently weren't too far away because they were able to restore order within twenty minutes, which seemed like an eternity in real-time.

I learned later that the family and friends attending the funeral had taken cover on the ground the entire time. Bullets hit the hearse and even the casket, but not one person was hit. That was only because the drug gang had not intended to hit anyone. Those gangs were good enough with their weapons that they could have taken out anyone they wanted. The gang was sending a message to another drug gang in the community that its days were numbered.

Of course, none of us knew that at the time when we resumed the funeral. Only a few people had left because of the gunfire. I preached the sermon while looking around to see if any more trouble would break out.

That was one of the fastest sermons I have ever preached. I was getting ready to high-tail it out of the cemetery when I was informed the presiding minister was required to witness the complete burial of the casket. I stood by the gravesite, keeping a watch on the area, and encouraging the workers to shovel faster.

When the men finished their job, I walked as fast as possible to my truck, got in, and locked the door. I released a huge sigh. Being inside my truck was the safest I had felt since the sound of the first shot.

Two blocks from the cemetery, I looked into my rear-view mirror and noticed a motorcycle with two armed men right on my bumper.

Just great!

The next traffic light was red as I approached, and I gradually slowed, hoping I wouldn't have to come to a complete stop. It didn't work out that way, and the motorcycle pulled up next to the driver-side window. I ducked to the floor of my truck.

I expected to hear gunfire, but instead, I heard a knock on my window.

"Pastor Eric!" came a voice.

Cautiously, I sat up and saw both men laughing big time. They were laughing so hard that they had to gather themselves to talk. They told me Frank had sent them to tell me that he wanted me to come back to meet with him. I told the men that I didn't feel safe going back into Castle City so soon after the pandemonium at the cemetery, but they assured me they would ride along with me on their motorcycle and keep me safe. Still, I convinced them to call Frank and ask him to meet me at a bakery inside the community, a more neutral location. They made the arrangements with Frank and still were laughing as we turned to head back into Castle City.

On our way into the community, an armored car joined us—which both helped and hurt with the fear I was feeling. Having the armored car and the armed men on the motorcycle made me feel safer, but it also reminded me of the seriousness of the risk factor.

I was signaled to park my truck once we made it into Castle City, then told to hop behind the driver of a waiting motorcycle. Another motorcycle with two armed men joined our group. The streets around the bakery had been shut down, and Frank was the only person inside.

Frank wouldn't look me in the eyes when I sat at his table. Tears streamed down his cheeks. His voice trembled as he spoke.

"The fellow you buried today was like a big brother to me. I want to thank you for what you did and tell you I'm sorry for what happened."

He pulled a roll of bills out of his pocket and laid it on the table. The bill on the outside of the roll was a U.S. $100 bill.

"What is this?" I asked.

"Take off the rubber band," Frank responded. I counted thirty $100 bills.

"Is that enough?" he asked.

"You don't need to pay me," I told him. "Yesterday when eleven people gave their lives to Jesus Christ, that was my payment."

"But it is our tradition to take care of the man who takes care of our man," Frank explained.

I couldn't take his money. I explained that according to the policy of my missions organization, I was paid to serve in Brazil and could only accept small amounts for speaking engagements when I was back home in the States. More important, I would never do anything in Brazil that could create the impression I could be bought.

"Please hear me, Frank," I said, wanting to make sure I didn't offend him. "God called me to Brazil and has provided for me. I don't need this money."

"Pastor, take the money and use it for your ministry," he pleaded with me. "Just take the money!"

Neither of us said anything for a few moments.

"If I took this money," I told him, "I would violate the oath I took to my missions agency and would be forced to return to the States."

"But how would they know?"

"The ministry money that I use is provided by them. If I minister without using their money, they will know something is not right."

Then I took a new angle with Frank.

"Do you think I love God?" I asked.

"No question about that."

"Do you think I love the community of Castle City?"

"No question."

"Do you want me to be here?"

"No question."

"Well, if I take that money," I told him, "I won't be around here anymore."

With that, Frank removed the money from the table. "I am indebted to you."

"Fine," I said. "If being indebted to me means that I can come back to preach the gospel, then we are all equal. Amen?"

Frank gave me a high five. We hugged, and I left to return home happy to be alive and reaching souls for Christ.

Followed

I wish that I could say I endured some fear-creating circumstances early during my time in Brazil and then learned to operate without experiencing fear. But that's not true. Learning to handle fear was an ongoing process for me.

Eight years after we had moved to Brazil, I encountered a situation that almost caused me to cancel a couple of weeks' worth of commitments in a church.

Our team had determined to make a concerted ministry effort in the *favelas* of Big Canoe and Santa Lucas. Our eventual goal was to start new churches there, and as part of that effort, I committed to conducting evangelism training in that area on Wednesday nights.

The host church was more than an hour's drive from our home, and enroute to that church on the second Wednesday, I noticed two young men behind me on a motorcycle. They seemed to be following me, and to find out if they were, I sped up, slowed down, changed lanes—anything to avoid a normal driving pattern. The motorcycle stayed with me through every maneuver.

I decided to stop at a gas station to see what would happen. When I pulled in, the motorcycle continued along. I bought a bottle of water and waited about ten minutes. Stopping would make me late to the training session, but I had to make sure I was safe. Shortly after resuming my trip, the two men on the motorcycle reappeared behind me. I prayed for God to cover my truck with the blood of Jesus through which no weapon could pass, then started singing the hymn, "Blessed Assurance."

> *Blessed assurance, Jesus is mine!*
> *Oh, what a foretaste of glory divine!*
> *Heir of salvation, purchase of God,*
> *Born of His Spirit, washed in His blood.*
>
> *This is my story, this is my song,*
> *Praising my Savior all the day long;*
> *This is my story, this is my song,*
> *Praising my Savior all the day long.*

Despite the motorcycle in the rear-view mirror, a sense of calm took over the inside of my truck.

I made it to the church and apologized for being a few minutes late. The training session went well, and at the end, without offering any explanation, I asked the group to pray for me. We prayed and then ate a meal the church had prepared for me.

I started back home at about 10 p.m. As soon as I pulled onto the highway, the same motorcycle with what looked to be the same two men was on my tail again.

The route home included a tunnel through a mountain, and as I approached—as *we* approached—I thought how the tunnel could be the perfect place for them to pull off an assassination. As I had on the trip in, I began singing again.

> *There is a name I love to hear,*
> *I love to sing its worth;*
> *It sounds like music in mine ear,*
> *The sweetest name on earth.*
>
> *Oh, how I love Jesus,*
> *Oh, how I love Jesus,*
> *Oh, how I love Jesus,*
> *Because He first loved me!*

I wasn't just singing. I was belting it out.

I decided to spend the rest of the drive focusing on God and not the motorcycle. Not until I reached our neighborhood did I look to see if the motorcycle was following me. It was, and it continued past me when I turned into the entrance into our neighborhood. I had been followed every mile of the trip, coming, and going. But I had no idea why.

I considered canceling the third and fourth Wednesday sessions, but I didn't want to disappoint the host church. The people were excited about the evangelism training and the future we were envisioning for their communities, with new and growing churches reaching more and more people.

Plus, I knew that if I canceled, I would be operating out of fear.

What we fear, we elevate in status. What we elevate in status, we worship.

I decided instead to worship Jesus and trust Him to protect me as he had the previous Wednesday.

The next two Wednesdays, a motorcycle with two men followed me round-trip. I didn't make any stops either Wednesday, praying the entire time.

God, I'm here, called of You to train Your people and to share Jesus here. Father, I give these two men into Your hands. Save them so that they will know You. Touch their hearts this very moment.

Both Wednesday nights, I arrived home without incident but still had no clue why I was being tailed.

The same week that the final training session had been completed, I received a call from the manager of a nearby slum controlled by drug lords. The manager said he needed to see me right away and asked me to meet him at the sewage canal. That was a strange place to meet, but I agreed to the meeting.

Two men were there with him when I arrived.

"An incident has occurred," the manager told me. "Since you have been in this community for a long time, I want to explain this incident to you. You see, people can die when they mess with certain people."

The manager opened a yellow envelope to reveal a picture of Anthony, a Peruvian friend of mine and a dedicated missionary. Anthony was thirty-six and ministered in one of the *favelas*.

"Do you know this guy?" the manager asked.

"Yes."

"Well, he messed with the wrong people."

"In what way?"

The manager pulled another picture out of the envelope. It showed Anthony talking to the police at the police station. Then the manager reached into his pocket, pulled out a small tape recorder, and pressed the play button. I heard Anthony revealing information about the community to the police.

"It was reported that a missionary was leaking information to the police," the manager said. "Trackers were put on both you and Anthony."

That explained the men on motorcycles.

The three men backed up a few feet and turned to look down into the canal. I stepped forward and saw Anthony's body in the sewage.

Anthony and I had been friends for four years. On the first day he arrived in Rio, I had warned him about remaining neutral in the community.

"You don't see anything, hear anything, or say anything except that Jesus saves. Stay focused on the gospel," I advised him.

I cried as I continued to look down at Anthony's body.

What was he thinking? Who took those pictures? How was the conversation recorded? Why didn't he listen to me?

The manager interrupted my thoughts. "Pastor, you are a good pastor here. You don't have anything to worry about, so don't cry."

"I'm weeping for your salvation," I said.

The three men thought I was referring to what would happen to them when the police learned of Anthony's murder, but that wasn't it. I was weeping because the people who killed Anthony needed Jesus.

I returned home with a heavy heart. Emotionally, I was drained, partially because of being followed on the Wednesday trips. I had likely been spied on more times than I realized. I e-mailed two of my missions leaders to inform them that for the first time in many years, a missionary had been killed in the slums. Strangely enough, however, I believed the manager when he said that I didn't need to worry about my own life.

I performed Anthony's funeral, and many from his community attended. Tragic deaths tended to come with a silver lining in the *favelas* because they were a wake-up call for the people. During the service, some non-Christians accepted Christ, and some believers rededicated themselves to Him. I took note of three people in attendance to whom I had witnessed before, who had come to Christ through Anthony's ministry.

Anthony's life was cut far too short in my eyes, but his life had not been lived in vain.

Fear is thick in the *favelas*, and I was by no means exempt from having to deal with it. It was a constant companion. Did I fear for my life? You bet. By living and working in the evil environment of the *favelas*, I stayed one poor decision by another person from eternity in heaven. I was literally living on the edge of eternity.

I have yet to find in the Bible where Jesus said, "If you have bullets flying around you or armed men following you, don't share the gospel. I was not going to allow those men to prevent me from doing what I went to Rio to do. Regardless of the obstacles and how many I encountered; the gospel had to get to those people.

From Ramona's prayer journal:

"Lord, you have not given us a spirit of fear but of power, love, and a sound mind. May my husband walk in your power, love, and sound mind right now—wherever he stands at this moment. In Jesus's name. Amen."

Chapter 11

Relying on God's Sufficient Grace

If I had surveyed *favela* residents and asked their top priority for their communities, the top answer would have been their security. It would not have been sanitation or even health—and both were extremely important issues in the slums. But more than anything, the residents wanted to live in a secure neighborhood.

The most difficult part of my job was the security risk in the slums. I like adrenaline, and I spent a lot of my days running on it. I was often asked, because of the dangerous environment in the *favelas*, if I lived under pressure and tension. I didn't. I did, however, maintain a constant awareness of my surroundings. My military background came in handy.

When I visited the barbershop and talked with the men there, when I checked in on business owners in their stores, or when I was involved in any other routine daily activities in the slums, I made a note of a spot I could duck into for safety if something crazy started happening. When I was driving up a mountainside, I scouted out curves and places alongside the road in case I needed to exit my truck and head for cover. While we were in Rio, the number of cement homes and buildings in the *favelas* increased. More cement meant more places I could dive behind if needed.

I did not allow fear of what could happen to preoccupy my mind, but I did keep tabs on the environments of the *favelas*. I read the local papers daily to keep up with what was taking place in the communities, and friends provided me with word-on-the-street updates.

I kept an updated "risk rate" chart for the communities we ministered in. The scale ran from one to ten. Ten was the most dangerous, with people dying every week in violence. A five, by comparison, meant unrest in a *favela*, such as an opposing group that wanted to come in and take over by force or the presence of inner fighting. When an area rated at least a five, I kept my wife and daughters out of that community. At a rating of eight, I pulled out until that area cooled off.

I intentionally remained neutral at all times. I did not choose sides and avoided anything that could make it appear I favored a particular side. Still, I had officials who knew me and our work, who did get word to me when things were about to start hopping and that we should stay out of their community.

The only problem with the risk-rate grades was that a

community's grade could jump dramatically in a heartbeat—sometimes when I was inside the community.

That happened once in a *favela* that was a 3.5 on my chart. I took my youngest daughter, Alicia, who was five then, into the community with me when I was to speak at a church event honoring a national who had helped our ministry a great deal.

During the ceremony, we heard gunfire outside, and when the event concluded, I told Alicia, "We need to get out of here" in a tone equal parts "Everything is okay" and "Get to the truck—now."

I was driving down the road when I heard more rapid gunfire.

Pow, pow, pow!

It sounded like the back of my truck had been hit.

Oh, Jesus, help us, I prayed.

Trying to remain calm, I suggested that Alicia lie down in the back seat. I started driving faster. Much faster. It was nighttime, and I was having a difficult time locating the route to the main highway out of the community.

I sensed the Lord telling me to reduce my speed. We approached a bus stop, and I saw three guys sitting there, I assumed, waiting for the bus. I turned on the dome light inside my truck so the men could see me—and specifically that my hands were holding nothing but the steering wheel—as I pulled up alongside them.

"Excuse me," I said to get their attention. "I'm an American missionary, and I was just preaching at a church. How can I get to the highway?"

As I finished my question, I noticed one of the men holding an AK-47.

"Oh, you're that missionary guy!" the man with the gun said. "Come follow us. Let's get you out of here really quick because things are jumping up right now."

The three men led me, with my sleeping daughter, to the highway, and I can't tell you how grateful I was that the Lord had slowed me down so I could see the men who would take us to safety.

A Church of Courage

The pastor of a congregation in the slum of Santa Lucas invited me to preach during a special event for his church. Several murders had recently occurred in the community, and the pastor wanted me to encourage his people not to be fearful. He told me the theme of the event: "Men of God who are not fearful."

Based on the title, I wasn't sure I was the best choice to speak, but I accepted his invitation anyway.

A young seminary student named John accompanied me. His job, while I preached, was to pray because I knew we were going into a dangerous community. When we arrived, I observed the event was bigger than I had been led to expect.

John and I were handed T-shirts that read *Homens de Coragem* ("Men of Courage") on the front. I was told the event would last all night and into the morning, from 7:30 p.m. to 5:00 a.m. About fifty or sixty men, wearing *Homens de Coragem* shirts, and a few women made their way into the church.

I preached on a familiar story—David and Goliath. I had three main points I wanted to make.

The first was that men of God who stand for God are not afraid to fight for God. I explained the point. "If someone came to me to say that Jesus is not Lord, I would stand my ground and be willing to say that He *is* Lord. I would be willing to fight for what is true."

As soon as I said that gunshots erupted from out in the community.

The only person who hit the deck was the guest-speaking American missionary invited to tell the locals that men of God are men of courage. John laughed out loud. I looked out from my prone position to see smiles across the congregation. I stood up, apologized, and resumed preaching.

My second point was that David carried with him memories of being willing to fight for the right.

King Saul told David he was too young to fight Goliath, yet David told Saul how when he was a young shepherd, he killed a lion and a bear that threatened his sheep.

As if on cue, shots rang out again. This time, though, they came from a machine gun. And this time, the bullets hit the church building. One bullet went through the top of a wall and hit a ceiling fan in the sanctuary. Again, I hit the deck. This time, I wasn't alone. The entire congregation dived onto the floor to avoid potential crossfire coming through the windows.

The front doors to the church also served as the front doors to the sanctuary. With no foyer or lobby, only the doors separated the sanctuary from outside. I looked toward the two doors right as a man's hand reached through one. Then the hand fell hard to the floor.

A member of the congregation crawled to the doorway and saw that the man was dead from a gunshot to the head. The dead man's mother was in the sanctuary, and when she learned her son had died, she wailed hysterically. Some of the ladies took her to a Sunday school room so she wouldn't have to see her son's body.

I had heard gunshots many times while preaching or sitting in a church, but I had never witnessed anyone die at the church door. The fear I felt in that sanctuary was as pure as any fear I had ever felt. But as had happened many times when I experienced fear, God's peace overcame me in a way stronger than the fear.

I walked over to talk to John, whose eyes revealed his fear. He looked at me, visibly shaken, and said, "You are called to the ministry. You are an old man, but I am a young man who has a lot of life in front of me. I do not want to be a part of your team after tonight!"

I had no response for John. We have kept in touch with John, and he is a faithful and active member of his church. But what we did in Rio was not for him, and that was fine. He wasn't the first person I'd heard say something similar in Rio, and I didn't try to convince anyone to "just hang in there and give it another try."

My belief is that people have to be called by God to do what we do. If they joined our ministry on their own plan, it usually didn't take them long to figure out they wouldn't be able to cut it. I didn't look down on them or lecture them or try to discourage them in any way. I remained their friend and did what I could to help them find their place for ministry. John had recognized he couldn't handle it, and in those circumstances, that was certainly understandable.

With one man having died at the door and his mother in a room screaming, I figured the event faced a premature ending. As I wondered when it would be safe for John and me to return to my truck and head home, the pastor got up at the front of the church and announced, "Pastor Eric now will finish his message."

Pastor Eric will now do what? Pastor Eric is ready to go home!

Quietly I said to the pastor, "I don't know. Do you think this is—"

"Come on and finish the message, Pastor!" he interrupted. "God is using you!"

With much hesitation—and with fear mixed in, too—I returned to the pulpit and picked up with point three: the battle was not David's, it was the Lord's.

"I can present myself in front of a giant," I said to the congregation, "but if I'm going to win, I am going to need God's help. But we don't need God's help if we are not standing in front of a giant in the first place."

You might have a difficult time believing this, but I'll call God as my witness that at the end of my third point, gunfire broke out yet again. Everyone scrambled to the floor, and we stayed there as the gunfire continued for at least five minutes. Between shots, I heard a body drop just outside the doorway. A man in the church crawled over to peek out.

Another man had been killed within arm's length of the young man whose body still lay at the church doors. The second victim was the brother of a woman who attended the church. His sister fainted. I helped take her to the same Sunday school classroom where the mourning mother still was being attended to.

I sat down in a moment of silence, and it struck me that when both dead members of the drug gang had been shot, they were trying to get into the church for refuge. Tears started flowing from my eyes at the thought of two men killed so close to a place that could have saved them in more ways than one.

The pastor came over and told me that he had shared the gospel with the first young man a week earlier, but that the man had not been interested.

"I wish I had done more," the pastor said several times.

All I could do was encourage the pastor by telling him to remember that he had done his best and that God's Word never returns void. The pastor broke down crying.

A woman behind us cried out, "Does God love us?"

By 2:30 in the morning, morgue representatives had removed the bodies, and the police had wrapped up their interviews. Only one person had left the church, and it wasn't John. It was the minister who was supposed to preach after me. He'd had enough and high-tailed it out of there.

Knowing the pastor had planned a longer event, I volunteered to preach some more—same theme, but a different message.

The congregation, stunned by the events, began singing "Amazing Grace." There wasn't one dry eye in the place. I took my place at the front of the church again and recited Psalm 30:5, reminding the people that "… weeping may endure for a night, but joy comes in the morning" (NKJV).

I turned to 1 Corinthians 13 to start a new sermon in my attempt to answer the question the woman had cried out earlier: "Does God love us?" The answer, I told the people, was in the cross. That was where we saw the love of God. Even while we were God's enemies, He loved us by sending Christ to die for us.

I concluded with a question for the congregation: "Who here tonight will share, with those outside, that God loves them?"

Everyone in the sanctuary stood and moved to the front of the church. Many were crying as they came forward.

After a time of prayer at the front, I walked to the church doors and looked outside. It was 4:30 in the morning. After a night of high emotions inside, a few policemen had been posted in the area, and everything finally appeared calm outside. The pastor came over to me, and I asked if he thought we could prayer-walk around the known drug-selling points.

We asked who in the congregation would join us, and almost everyone still there committed to going. We left the building praying and singing. At one of our stops, the pastor prayed loudly and with authority that God would close down the selling points.

Two weeks after the event, the pastor called me. His church's congregation had doubled in size, he said, and he asked if I would come back to train his people in evangelism. I asked why more people were coming to the church, and he explained that when residents in the neighborhood had seen us praying and singing in the streets, they thought we were brave.

"They thought it was bravery that allowed us to prayer-walk through the community," he told me. "But it wasn't bravery—it was our faith in God."

When I returned for the training, the inside of the church was standing room only.

Six months later, the paramilitary stormed into Santa Lucas and removed or killed the drug dealers. The community became drug-free, and the church had so many people in attendance that it required two services to hold them all.

Up to My Neck

In addition to being shot, I also fear contracting a deadly disease. Again, Rio was not a good place to live with that fear.

I once came upon a girl who had been beaten, and I did the first thing that came to mind—picked her up and hurriedly carried her to a hospital. In the process, the girl's blood got all over me. The girl died from her wounds, and because I had taken her to the hospital, I was informed that the girl had AIDS.

To make sure I hadn't picked up HIV from her, I had to undergo six monthly tests. I felt like my life had been put on hold throughout the testing. Learning that the final test came back negative and being cleared by the doctors was a tremendous relief because a state of uncertainty had hung over me the entire six months.

It's one thing when a violent situation breaks out without warning, and your adrenaline picks up, and you enter into a life-or-death survival mode. But it is completely different—a helpless feeling—when you wonder every day whether a life-threatening disease is inside you, silent and unseen, plotting an attack against you. I think I worked three times harder during that testing period to keep my mind occupied.

That scare caused me to become more cautious about coming into contact with other people's blood. When I encountered someone bleeding while I was wearing a long-sleeved shirt with the sleeves rolled up, I pulled the sleeves all the way down and buttoned them. I put on gloves, too, before I touched the person.

In one instance, both of my big fears confronted me.

Someone informed me of an elderly woman in Canal Vale who desperately needed help. She had some type of illness, and her family, fearful of catching whatever disease she had, abandoned her in an old wooden shack. The woman was lying there, alone and dying.

Canal Vale was a drug-run community at the time, and I asked my friend Marcos to escort me into the slum and help me locate the shack. My goal was to help the woman while getting into and out of Canal Vale as quickly as possible.

We decided to take a side road into Canal Vale because I knew my truck would be recognized on that side of the slum. With Marcos's help, we found the shack. I parked alongside. The shack sat next to the local sewage pond, and the only thing that smelled worse than the nearby *esgoto* was the inside of the shack.

The only light in the shack came from outside, through the cracks between the pieces of wood. The elderly woman was barely breathing, lying on a mat coated with her own waste. She was so weak that she didn't move when we entered. All she could do was follow our movements with her eyes. Based on what I had been told, Marcos and I estimated that she had been there, uncared for, up to a week. I got down onto the floor and leaned my ear to her chest. I could barely detect a heartbeat. Marcos found a piece of scrap plastic and covered the back seat of my truck.

Her back was plastered with waste, so Marcos and I put on rubber gloves to clean her back before carrying her to my truck. Marcos persuaded a reluctant teenage girl nearby to help us. I held the woman up in a sitting position while the girl began cleaning her back. The mess the woman had been lying in was a sickening sight, and I admired the girl for helping.

We found some cleaner clothes, and Marcos and I stepped out of the shack and removed our gloves while the girl changed the woman's clothes inside. The girl told us the woman's back was covered with sores.

Marcos had to leave for work, and as the girl was finishing inside, a motorcycle sped past. The two men on board were waving pistols, and one was yelling, *"O cara! O cara! O cara!"* A second motorcycle with two more men was close behind them. The passenger carried an AK-47 and a bag.

The second motorcycle hit a bump at a high rate of speed, and a thick roll of money flew out of the passenger's coat pocket. When the men didn't stop to pick up the money, I knew we were in the middle of a bad scene.

The local girl told me *"O cara!"* meant "The man," or that the police were coming. The girl and I picked up our pace to get out of there before the police arrived.

We went back into the rancid shack and were carrying the woman to the door when we heard a bullet hit one of the walls. In a sequence I can still see in slow motion, I saw the bullet hole in the wall, we dropped to the floor, and I looked to the teenage girl as she started screaming.

I crawled to the door and looked outside just in time to see a bullet shatter the back window on the passenger side of my truck's cab. Then another bullet whistled through the shack.

God, please don't let this girl get hit, I prayed. *Please don't let me get hit, and please don't let this lady die on the floor.*

Between the girl's persistent screams, I heard two more bullets hit my truck.

I hoped that whoever was shooting would hear the girl and know someone was in the shack. But that didn't seem to be working. I spotted a scrap of white cloth and tied it to the end of a stick to make a "surrender" flag. I looked over to the girl and the woman and saw a pool of blood next to the girl. She had been shot in her left foot.

From what I had learned in the military, I grabbed an old shirt, tore it, and with a small stick, placed a tourniquet on the girl's foot to stop the bleeding—being very careful, of course, not to allow any of her blood to touch my skin.

I dipped my white flag into the pool of blood on the floor, crawled through the door to my truck, and—staying as low as possible—waved the flag over my head.

Two bullets flew through my surrender flag.

I also noticed that the right rear tire on my truck had been shot out, too.

The shootout between the police and the drug dealers showed no sign of ending soon. An elderly woman with a faint heartbeat, and a girl with a gunshot wound, were inside the shack, and it was almost dark. I knew that I needed to find some way of making it known that innocent people were in the line of fire.

I lay down behind my truck to look around. I saw the *esgoto* close by and decided that if I could make it to the other side of the pond, I could get help.

I rolled down the short embankment from the shack to the sewage. I didn't think I had been seen, so I stood to my feet and hunched over. The sewage/water level was just below my knees. The smell was nauseating.

Staying low, I started running through the shallow water along the edge of the pond. The pond eventually grew deeper. At one point, I waded through water neck high while looking for a safe place to exit the pond.

Now I wish I had thought of Isaiah 43:2, which begins, "When you pass through the waters, I will be with you; and through the rivers, they shall not overflow you …" (NKJV).

Finally, I noticed the main sewage canal. I crawled out of the canal and onto dry land. I was greeted by the sound of guns cocking.

Facedown on the ground, I looked up to see several policemen with guns pointed directly at me. One put his boot on my neck and ordered me not to move.

"I am an American missionary," I said. (Have you noticed how many times that line has worked for me?)

The policeman lifted his foot off my neck and told me to remove everything from my pockets. All I had to show them was my truck keys.

With guns still pointed at me, the questions began. The policemen thought I was a drug dealer.

Out of God's grace, a man I knew walked by. "Pastor Eric!" he called out. It had been a while since I'd been so happy to hear my name called like that.

When my friend called me "Pastor," the policemen lowered their guns.

"Do you know this guy?" the sergeant asked the passerby.

"Yes," he answered. "He is an American missionary and helps out in this community."

The police, satisfied with the man's identifying me, allowed me to stand. I began telling the story of how I ended up in the canal and that the girl and the elderly woman in the shack needed immediate medical assistance.

The sergeant sent two of his men to the shack.

All I wanted to do at that point was go home. But first, one of the officers insisted that I be hosed down to get the sewage off of me, so they did that.

The police also wanted to move my truck for me, but I was concerned that if the drug dealers saw police near my truck, they would think I was helping the police. I told the officers that I would return later, alone, for my truck. Then they offered to give me a ride home in one of their police cars. Again, I didn't want to risk being associated with the police, so I told them I would walk to the next community and get a motorcycle taxi to take me home from there.

Before I left, the sergeant told me that because I had been in the sewage, I was at risk of being infected with hepatitis. Just what I needed to hear to cap off that day.

By that point, I most wanted a hot shower and a stiff scrub brush, so I changed my mind about walking and catching a motorcycle taxi. I asked if an officer in an unmarked car could give me a ride home.

At home, I scrubbed every inch of my body in the shower for forty-five minutes.

I had left the community believing the police would take care of the girl and woman, but I later learned that they had not been rescued from the shack until around 1 a.m.

The girl had lost a lot of blood from the gunshot wound, but she recovered in the hospital. The elderly woman also survived. When the area drug boss learned that the woman had almost died during the shootout, he had her shack torn down and replaced with a small, cement home. The last I knew, the woman still lived there with one of her sons, who cared for her. She was healthy with ongoing treatment.

I had to sweat out six more months of blood tests, this time for hepatitis. Once again, with all praise to God, I received a clean bill of health.

Safe and Secure

The angels who protected me had to work overtime sometimes. I'm glad they were willing to put in the extra work.

The writer of Psalm 91 was grateful for his angels, too. That psalm is a wonderful presentation of what it's like to possess the security that comes from living under God's protection. Verses 4-6, especially, stand out to me:

> *He shall cover you with His feathers,*
> *And under His wings you shall take refuge;*
> *His truth shall be your shield and buckler.*
> *You shall not be afraid of the terror by night,*

Nor of the arrow that flies by day,
Nor of the pestilence that walks in darkness,
Nor of the destruction that lays waste at noonday (NKJV).

Bullets have been my arrow, and HIV and hepatitis have been my pestilence. I know of many Christians, including missionaries, who have been victims of "arrows" and "pestilence." Bad things happen to people doing the work of the Lord. I don't have an answer for the "Why?" questions, which, by the way, I have asked many times. I know only that the grace of God is sufficient for me every day.

That is why I declare the words of the psalmist in verse 2: "He is my refuge and my fortress; My God, in Him will I trust."

From Ramona's prayer journal:
"Lord, thank You that you give Your angels charge over Reese and let no harm come to him."

Chapter 12

Faith Conquers Fear

The apostle John begins his gospel by writing, "In the beginning was the Word, and the Word was with God, and the Word was God" (NKJV). John goes on to add that Jesus was present at creation and as the source of all life was "the light of men." In verse 5, John writes, "And the light shines in the darkness, and the darkness did not comprehend it." The word "comprehend" can be translated as "overcome."

The darkness of evil never has and never will overcome the light.

For Christians living in the *favelas*, however, it was easy to believe the darkness of evil was too dark for the light of the gospel.

One of the primary challenges for pastors in the slums was to get their people inside the church to carry the light outside into the community and to keep the doors open wide so that those on the outside could see the light and be drawn inside.

That was a message easier preached than lived, for sure, but with

God and through God, all things are possible.

A church in Mount Azul could testify to that.

Mount Azul had become the most dangerous *favela* in Rio. A new drug faction had risen up and knocked out the existing drug lord and his dealers. The way into and out of Mount Azul had been blockaded so that the new regime could clean house in the community.

Everyone within the slum knew what was coming but was unable to flee.

The new ruling force went door to door within Mount Azul one night, searching for members of the old drug faction. When the members were found, they were dragged into dark streets and executed with a shot to the head. Their wives and children ran wailing into the streets and alleys. Chaos reigned, and the police could not break through the blockades. The police might have been too afraid of the new regime to attempt to end the violence.

When the night of murders was over, nineteen drug dealers and eleven innocent people had lost their lives.

Two months later, the pastor of the Mount Azul church asked me to preach to his congregation. In the wake of the devastating drug war, he wanted his people to be challenged to share with the community that hope could be found in Christ.

The invitation was for a Sunday evening. Ramona and the girls attended our family's church on Sunday mornings, even when I preached elsewhere. Because this would be a night service, my family could go with me to Mount Azul.

Gloria was my timekeeper. She made sure before we arrived that I understood we were to be out of the community by 9 p.m. Brazilian church services could run long, with two- or three-hour services common. Gloria also knew that the guest speaker had a reputation for getting a little long-winded when he got on a roll behind the pulpit. I told her not to worry that night, though, because I wanted to have my family out before nine o'clock.

By arrangement with the powers that controlled Mount Azul, a church member met us at the entrance to the community. He had been instructed to walk into the community ahead of our truck with a Bible held up to his chest. I was to drive slowly behind him with windows rolled down, and my truck's interior lights on so the snipers stationed along the route could see clearly into our vehicle.

I parked the truck when the road became too narrow to drive through, and with Ramona and the girls close beside me, we walked up the winding dirt street to the church. I knew we were being watched, and because I was wearing a suit and suits were often associated with politicians, I walked with my Bible in plain view. I wanted it clear that I was a preacher.

Before we entered the church, I was told that "We are surrounded by people who need Jesus" was church members' code phrase to alert others that drug dealers were around the church, and it was unsafe to leave the building.

All the rules and escorts and code phrases were put aside, though, when the service began.

About 150 people jammed into the wooden pews that weren't designed to comfortably hold that many. I was amazed at how the people who had witnessed and even lost so much in the previous two months could worship in such a powerful and focused manner.

I began my sermon with a question: "Have you heard the cry of the lost world? In Matthew 9:35–37, Jesus looked at the multitudes and saw sheep without a shepherd, people who were downcast and hopeless. But He was filled with compassion. If we are going to respond to the cry of a lost world, we need compassion. If you don't have compassion for lost people, you will not share the love of God with them."

This was my first time preaching in that church, and I always had a curiosity about how a congregation would respond my first time in front of them. I had a booming voice and liked to pace around the platform. After my opening remarks, I surveyed the crowd and was happy to see smiles throughout the congregation. So, I continued in my typical style.

"Before the service, a lady told me that the community is going from bad to worse. Sin can be confronted, but it must be confronted with love. When Jesus told the woman at the well to go get her husband, He knew that she had five previous husbands and was living with a sixth man who wasn't her husband. But He didn't blast her with what He knew. He told her gently and let her figure out that how she was living was not good.

"When another woman was going to be stoned for adultery, Jesus said, 'Let the one who has no sin cast the first stone.' When everyone left except Jesus and this woman, He asked her, 'Where are your accusers?' He didn't condemn her or point in her face angrily. Instead, He gently instructed, 'Neither do I condemn you, but go and sin no more.'"

The point I hoped the church would grasp was that the gun-toting drug dealers who had terrorized their community were human beings. Those confrontational carriers of evil could be confronted—with love. So could their wives and girlfriends. I added that I had spoken in love with drug dealers, prostitutes, and transvestites on many occasions, and I was standing up in front of the congregation still alive and sharing the gospel. If this man with feet of clay could do it, so could they.

"When you have compassion for people, you will pray for them," I continued. "And when you pray for them, God will show you what to say to them. The task is bigger than you, me, this church, and all the churches. But it is not too big for our God. There may be a gun around every corner in Mount Azul, but God is here, too. As you pray, God will show you how to do acts of kindness that will speak to those who do not know Him. Look at me—I have had a weapon pointed in my face nine times. Am I still here today?"

A woman in the congregation looked at the person next to her with a look I read to say, *No way—not me. I'm not doing that!*

That was the look I needed to see to keep on going.

"Yes, I have fears and doubts at times. But when those feelings come, I pray. Like the man in Mark 9:24 who said to Jesus, 'Lord, I believe; help my unbelief!' when your faith is weak, pray and ask God to make your faith stronger, to take your doubts away."

I was completely unaware that my sermon was being heard through speakers outside the church building. I was unashamedly declaring the truth, such as, "There is no authority in this community that is higher than the authority of Christ Jesus. The Bible says, 'Greater is He who is in you than he who is in the world.'"

Almost as soon as I finished those thoughts on "authority in the community," four-armed drug dealers stepped into the open doorway of the church.

The members of the congregation had their backs to the doorway, but I could see the men clearly from my vantage point—perhaps a little too clearly for my comfort level. I wasn't ready to ask just yet for their thoughts on who was the ultimate authority in the community.

The men turned and left the church, and I wrapped up my message and closed the service in prayer. It was 8:35 p.m., and my little timekeeper appeared antsy. I located the man who had escorted us into the community, but he pointed out that it was now dark out. I could tell he was leery of leading us back to our truck in the dark, so I let him off the hook.

When we reached our truck, one of my rear tires was sitting a little low. I was certain that wasn't because of a slow leak. But there was enough air in the tire to drive on it, so I slowly exited the community and stopped at the first gas station. It was nine o'clock when I aired up the tire. We were headed home on four good tires, and Gloria was happy.

Return Engagement

Six months passed without hearing from the pastor. I thought that strange, but I didn't make contact with him. He called me one day, though, not sounding too thrilled to be starting the conversation.

He reluctantly told me that I and my message had not been well received by his church. His people hadn't appreciated someone from outside of Mount Azul coming into their community and telling them they should be witnessing to drug dealers. As someone who didn't live in their war zone, they believed I had not earned that right, which made sense to me.

But what they did not know was that I had put my life on the line many times in other communities in the name of proclaiming the gospel. In fact, I had possibly put my life at risk—and even my family's—to come to their church! But still, I thought they had a legitimate reason for their feelings.

I'm sure they feared the new regime and didn't want to risk rocking the boat after things had calmed down (relatively speaking) following the night thirty people had been killed.

The pastor told me he had wanted me to return to preach at the church's upcoming anniversary celebration, but his leadership team had voted—unanimously, he added—that I not be invited. The pastor had then contacted other preachers who the leaders had recommended, but none would accept an invitation to Mount Azul.

Having struck out with the other speakers, the pastor received permission to invite me. The members said that at least I had been "animated and a good speaker."

That was the most tepid speaking invitation I had ever received, but I respected the pastor for going to bat for me with his leadership team and congregation. I said I would get back to him.

I was unsure I should accept because the people seemed like they would have closed ears toward me going into the celebration. I prayed and sensed the Lord giving me the go-ahead. I called the pastor and told him I would come, but for the Sunday evening service instead of the morning service.

When I told my family that I was going back to the Mount Azul church and that I was going on a Sunday evening, Gloria said, "May God bless you, but *I'm* not going!"

I thought her response was funny, but Ramona didn't laugh.

"Gloria, we need to support Daddy," she said.

Gloria reluctantly agreed to go, but she was even more adamant than usual about finishing by 9 p.m.

We drove to Mount Azul late on Sunday afternoon, and the same man met us at the community entrance to escort us. As he walked with his Bible in front of his chest and we followed in the truck, I noticed a new drug-selling point had been established up ahead, directly in front of the church. That got me a little riled up. Apparently, nothing was sacred to the new ruling drug faction.

I prayed out loud in my truck, "Jesus, would You protect us and lead me to say only what You want me to say? Would you bless these young men selling drugs right there and give them a divine revelation?"

We parked in the same place as before and walked the same narrow, dirt road to the church. But this time, we walked right past the new drug-selling point.

My boldness theme hadn't gone over too well on my previous visit, so this time I chose to preach on love. I figured, *who could argue with a sermon on God's love?* At least, I hoped that was the case.

Right up until the time I took the pulpit, I coached myself. *Reese, you will not talk loudly. They have speakers on the outside of the building, and you're gonna talk about love. You are not going to offend anyone by talking about love.*

I took my text from James with a key theme from his book: Faith without works is dead.

As Jesus' half-brother, James had a first-hand perspective on Jesus' ability to combine truth with love. James, I told the congregation, said that we could talk about love all we want, but it is not until we act lovingly that we truly are doing something that matters. I added what Jesus had said about there being no greater love than laying down our life for another.

Remembering how I had lacked credibility in dealing with fear in the congregation's eyes, I shared a story from my life.

"One day, I was sitting at a café in your community while I drank a bottle of water and rested for a few minutes. All of a sudden, gunfire started. Everyone, including me, ran to the bar for cover. About twenty-five minutes later, I was sitting outside but on the alert for hearing more shots. That's when I saw this little boy. I was thinking to myself, *Kid, where's your momma? Get out of the line of fire! We don't know when they're coming back for another shootout.*

"Then I saw a stray mother dog with her hanging breasts. She was skinny as everything, and there were several puppies around her. This kid sat down on a rock and picked up one of those puppies. He rubbed its little furry head, and he touched his nose to the puppy's nose. For a long time, that boy loved on that puppy. When he put that puppy down, sure enough, that dog followed him everywhere he went.

"When we love people as God loves us, they can't help but follow the Lord Jesus Christ. Even when things were chaotic in the street, the boy focused on loving that puppy. When we love the way Jesus loves, even when there's trouble all around us, people will respond. I can't understand why people who say they love Jesus would never tell anybody about the wonderful love that Jesus gives."

I was feeling it at that point. I had already blown off my own coaching to stay calm and not get loud. I could tell that the congregation actually was feeling it this time, too, so I asked that everyone turn to the next person and say, "Jesus loves you, and so do I." They all did so with enthusiasm.

With the crowd on my side, I decided to push the envelope.

"Do you know who else Jesus loves?" I asked. "Jesus loves the prostitutes! If Rahab, the prostitute in Jericho who was saved by Joshua, were here tonight, and if I asked her if God loves prostitutes, she will say, 'Yes! He loved me and changed me and gave me courage!' What do you think Daniel and his three Hebrew friends would say if they visited us tonight?"

I motioned beside me as if the four were standing with me on the stage.

"Would they say that God loved them when they got in trouble with the king of Babylon? They would say, 'Are you serious? Yes! He delivered us after we stood up for Him.'"

I looked from my four imaginary friends and back over the congregation.

"Be not deceived, church. If God did something for someone else, He can do it for you. There are pregnant women in this community who do not know who got them pregnant, but God loves them. We in the church may want to condemn them, but if they cry out to God, He will absolutely forgive them. Can I get an 'Amen?'"

I didn't get *an* amen—I got amens from throughout the church.

This was the same congregation and the same speaker who hadn't connected six months earlier. God was definitely doing something among us that night.

I stopped my sermon right there. Certain they had gotten the point. I felt nothing more needed to be said. The congregation began singing a song called "Big Is Our God." While they were singing, I looked out to the congregation and saw a number of people peering inside through the double doors. I looked over to the pastor, wondering if he saw the same thing. He looked a little nervous.

Then someone with a 9mm pistol strapped to his waist walked in. He was one of the drug dealers, and his pregnant girlfriend was alongside him.

They began walking down the center aisle. The farther they proceeded down the aisle, the lower the congregation's singing voices became. It was as though with each row the couple passed, that row noticed them. The growing restlessness inside the church followed the couple until, by the time they reached the front, there wasn't a note being sung. The church was as quiet as a cemetery.

The drug dealer perked up as though a realization had settled in on him. He turned, ran back up the aisle, and handed his gun to someone standing at the door. As he started back down the aisle to join his girlfriend, the congregation resumed its song.

When I got a good look at the man, I recognized him as one of the dealers I had prayed for after seeing the new selling point. Even though he had handed over his gun, I wasn't sure yet whether this was an answer to prayer. When he spoke for the first time, I had my answer.

The man asked the pastor—the really nervous pastor—to pray for his pregnant girlfriend's baby. Then he asked the pastor to pray that God would help him stop dealing drugs! (I later learned the man actually was one of the main leaders of the drug faction controlling Mount Azul.)

The pastor asked the congregation if there were others who also wanted prayer. People streamed toward the altar, including from the crowd outside the church, too. As dozens of people stood alongside the couple and filled the front of the church, I glanced over to the pastor and caught a priceless look of his being overwhelmed at what God was doing in front of him.

The congregation that had previously lacked the courage to demonstrate love toward its drug-dealing enemies was embracing one who had courageously asked for help.

The church at Mount Azul learned an important lesson that I had learned through countless run-ins with fear during my years in Rio: faith conquers fear.

The Mount Azul congregation did not have to be afraid of sharing the gospel with the drug dealers of their community. God can speak—He wants to speak—even to those we would rather not mess with because it *can* get messy. It can be difficult. Sometimes, even dangerous. But God is no respecter of persons. He loves us and shows compassion to the multitudes, and He uses us to show His love and compassion to them.

From Ramona's prayer journal:
"Father, may we, Your people who are called by Your name, humble ourselves, pray, seek Your face, and repent, as 2 Chronicles 7:14 says. Thank You, Lord, for giving each of us a measure of faith. May we use that faith to please You and to lead others to Your Son, Jesus Christ. And Lord, protect my husband as he continues to lead us in this way in this place."

Eric Reese

Chapter 13

Anger that Motivates

I've said I have feet of clay and dating back to my last trip through college when I finally made a commitment to Christ that stuck, I had done a good job of controlling my anger. Remember, in my less civil days, I was enough of a fighter to earn my "Mike Tyson" nickname.

Soon after arriving in Brazil, I received a quick lesson on the importance of relying on the Holy Spirit to keep my emotions in check.

Ramona and I spend our first year in Brazil learning Portuguese at language school in Campinas, São Paulo. Ramona learned the language much quicker than I. When I tried my Portuguese on the street, the locals laughed at me. I hadn't anticipated the difficulty of ministering to people in their language, and my eagerness to begin sharing the gospel was well ahead of my mastery of Portuguese.

Wade Akins, a fellow missionary, helped me learn enough street language that I felt comfortable taking a chalkboard into the streets and evangelizing with a mix of preaching and drawing pictures. I made one request of the Lord: *Please don't let anyone ask me any questions because I don't think I know enough Portuguese to answer them. Or probably even understand their questions.*

One day I was preaching in a park when a Muslim preacher and his friends interrupted me by getting up in my face and screaming. I raised my hand, and one of the men slapped it down. Where I grew up, that would have been enough to spark an all-out fight.

Then one of them spat in my face. I felt the old Mike Tyson rising up within me. I'd punched people larger than the spitter and knocked them down with one punch. I wouldn't have even needed to take a full swing to knock that guy down.

But instead of striking back, I began saying to myself; *Eric is a Christian, Christian, Christian. He is a preacher, preacher, preacher, called to be a missionary, missionary, missionary. You've just gotta pray, pray, pray.*

I prayed, wiped the spit off my face, and asked the man to step back. My lack of emotional response upset him further.

At that moment, two other missionaries in language school with us stepped up and threatened to report the men to the policemen within shouting distance of us. The hecklers turned and left.

That incident was a reminder of how my flesh needed to always be under the control of the Holy Spirit. If I had acted out what would naturally come to me in that situation, Ramona and I would have been home in the States before we even finished language school.

That day also gave me a preview of how preaching the cross would be offensive to some. The way the two fellow missionaries brought an end to the situation taught me the importance of having teammates and co-workers around me. Because of that, when our team splits up as we went out to evangelize, no one went out alone.

Street Kids

There's the type of anger—personal anger—that the Holy Spirit suppressed in the park, but there was a different anger I consistently dealt with as I ministered—anger at situations. When I witnessed how street kids in Rio were treated, for example, righteous anger boiled up in me. Instead of causing me to want to strike someone, it caused me to reach out to the kids in love.

Jesus held a special place in His heart for children. His disciples discovered that when they rebuked parents who were bringing their children to Jesus to be blessed by Him. Mark 10:14 says Jesus became indignant: "When Jesus saw this, he was *indignant*. He said to them, 'Let the little children come to me, and do not hinder them, for the kingdom of God belongs to such as these'" (NKJV, emphasis mine).

If I could have seen Jesus' face as He walked the streets with us and watched the orphaned kids living on the streets of Rio, I expect I would have seen that look of indignation on His face as Mark described. Thousands of street kids had to juggle tennis balls or wash car windows for money to survive, often huddling together and sniffing glue to stay both warm at night and numb to their situations.

Rio's upper class tends to see the street kids as a menace to society. A woman once told me that street kids were like wild horses needing to be tamed. I invited her to come with me to get to know some of those "wild horses." Of course, she never showed up. Her attitude toward the kids was typical.

Street kids often were blamed for crimes they were not always guilty of committing. When they did commit crimes, it was mostly theft because stealing was the only way many could obtain what they needed to stay alive. But some also were involved in prostitution, and usually not by their choice.

I recall a newspaper account of a twelve-year-old girl living on the streets. The journalist found the girl living under a bridge and asked why she was there. The girl's mom was a cocaine addict. Her mom entertained men at her home and sold sex with her daughter for a $5 bag of crack, so the girl ran away from home. The journalist asked how many men her mother had forced her to have sex with. Fifteen to twenty, the girl said. She was *twelve*—and she had been forced to have sex with more men than she'd had birthdays!

With thousands of homeless kids in Rio, there was no easy solution. Because many residents of Rio viewed the street-kids problem as messy, human nature was to want someone else to deal with the messy problems. It was much easier for those with the resources to at least reduce the problem to instead simply turn away and ignore it. Out of sight, out of mind.

The street children might have been out of sight for most of the public in Rio, but they were not out of God's sight.

We included outreach to street kids in Care Night, loading a van and my truck with hot dogs, chips, soft drinks, Bibles, and tracts. We aimed to feed their bodies and their souls and to befriend them. Because we typically ministered in the same areas, we built relationships with some of the kids over time.

David was one of those kids.

One night while we were setting up in the Flamengo district, David ran up to me and greeted me with a hug.

"Did you bring us treats tonight, Pastor?" he asked, flashing a big smile.

David always had that big smile that would draw our team in. I liked David a lot. He was the type of kid I would have liked to take home with me to raise.

I first met David soon after we started ministering in Rio when he was ten or eleven years old and about sixty pounds of skin and bones. His teeth were rotting. In other words, he looked like the typical street orphan we saw all too many of.

David's mother had died of AIDS. The aunt he lived with was a prostitute. He feared his aunt would make him have sex with men for money, so he ran away and joined a gang of street kids living under a train bridge.

David liked to be our helper, and he went out and helped us round up a bunch of kids who would receive a hotdog and Coke if they would come to hear me tell a Bible story.

"I want to tell you about one of the greatest kings in Israel's history," I began. "Does anyone know his name?"

Either no one did, or the kids were too shy to answer, so I answered my own question. "His name was David."

Our David grinned from ear to ear. The other boys snickered, but David ignored them and kept his smiling face zeroed in on me.

"You lie!" one of the kids shouted out at me. I tell you; those street kids didn't just give their trust away.

I continued my story, acting out every part, including how David had been a shepherd boy. Then how he had killed a lion and a bear to protect his sheep. Then how David loved God.

I heard one of the kids tell a member of our team, "Tell him to talk faster." That's what I deserved for preaching to kids while the hot dogs were in plain sight.

"David was king for forty years," I said. "Do any of you know someone named David around here?"

They all pointed to my buddy. I didn't think David could smile any bigger than he had during that story, but somehow, he found some extra face to stretch his smile over. The attention had made the boy's night.

I glanced at my watch as I was reaching the most important part of the story and noticed it was 1:45 a.m. The kids were hanging on my every word. I spoke at a few churches where I would have loved to have had these kids sitting in the congregation! (Perhaps I should take hot dogs and sodas when I speak at those types of churches.)

I told the kids that God had made a plan for King David's life, that He had made a plan for each of their lives too, and that God had sent me to Rio to tell them that God loves them. God had sent His Son, Jesus, into our world to show us His love and invite us to become part of God's family. And how Jesus always welcomed little kids when they wanted to talk to Him. Then how they, too, could know Jesus in their hearts.

One girl blurted out, "Is Jesus a *gringo*?"

"No," I said, trying not to chuckle. "God is a God of all people. He's not American—He's the God of the whole world."

"Does He understand Portuguese?" another girl asked.

I assured her that He could understand her.

Then I described for the kids Jesus' death and resurrection.

"You lie!" the untrusting boy again said.

"No, the Bible says Jesus died and rose again. If you believe that, you can ask Him to come and live in your heart. And I don't want you to do it just to get food. Everybody's going to get plenty of food in a minute. What's important is that God knows your heart. So, everyone—with your eyes closed—if you want to ask Jesus into your heart, raise your hand."

Several, including David, raised their hands.

Those kids repeated after me a prayer asking Jesus into their hearts, and then I leaned over to David. "Did you trust Jesus?"

"Yep."

"So, where is He now?"

"In heaven."

"Remember how you asked Him into your heart?"

"Yep."

"He is now in your heart. He is with you wherever you go."

"Yep, He is."

I looked up to see the kids begin scrambling in every direction. I had missed the police car easing past. A police car might have been a street kid's greatest fear.

One of our Brazilian team members had previously explained to me that sometimes the police picked up street kids, and then the kids were never seen again. A report by the United Nations in the 1980s said that street kids in Brazil were sometimes killed to get them off the streets.

The kids had sat through my message, but they had split before we handed out the hot dogs and Cokes. We moved to an area three blocks down the street to hand out food and drinks to transvestites, but we saved some of the hot dogs and Cokes for the kids, figuring they would come out of hiding when the coast was clear and find us to get the food we had promised.

Some of the kids did reappear for the food about an hour and a half later, but David wasn't one of them.

I couldn't get David out of my mind for the next two days, so I drove back into Flamengo to look for him. I asked a group of street kids if they knew where he was, and they pointed to a kid washing the windows of a car that stopped at an intersection. I waited for David while he finished the job, and then he came over to see me.

I asked him how we were doing. He replied that he was doing well, and I handed him a Bible.

He looked disappointed. "I don't read very well," he said.

I told him about a nearby church that would help him. Then I said goodbye to David.

I kept thinking about him for weeks. I checked with the pastor of the church I had recommended, and he hadn't seen him. Then, finally, I heard some good news. Another church that ministered to street kids had met David and taken him in. He wound up growing spiritually there.

David is no longer a street kid. Or even a kid. He's grown up now and pastors a Protestant church about forty-five minutes from Rio. David has not forgotten the environment his new life in Christ saved him from, and his church has a tremendous outreach to homeless kids.

Lesson From a Child

What do you say to a young boy who asks, "If there is a God, where was He when my stepfather was abusing me?"

The boy's name was Ian, and he was thirteen. I had finished talking to a group of street kids when Ian shouted his question for all to hear.

I had no answer to offer.

Instinctively, I walked up to Ian to give him a hug. He avoided my embrace. I hadn't even thought that a boy who had been physically abused by an adult male would want nothing to do with my attempted show of affection. His reaction made it clear that he had suffered tremendous pain.

"Ian, some people don't think God exists because of bad things that have happened," I told him. "There were also bad men in the Bible, but eventually there is going to be a payday. But we can't blame God for what God did not do."

He didn't say anything as I looked around and waited on the Holy Spirit to guide me on what to say next.

"Have any of these kids stolen things?" I asked.

"Yeah."

"What would happen if the police came and said you were with them, so they were going to charge you with stealing as well? Would that be right?"

"No."

"Well, then why is God being charged with what your stepfather did?"

Ian took a moment before answering, "I have heard you say that God is all-powerful, so why couldn't He step in during those three years I was abused?"

"God could have, but why didn't He? I wish I could give you an answer," I said. "But if you look at it that way, you will always be angry at God. You could say, 'My mom got married to a man who abused me, and he will receive punishment,' or you could look at it another way and say, 'Something happened to me that was very hurtful, and I pray to God that He would give me the strength to overcome what this bad man did to me.'"

"I can't separate that," he said with a pained expression. "It's not fair."

I could see some transvestites across the street walking around in their high heels and revealing outfits, doing their best to outdo the others in attracting the attention of passengers in the cars driving past their area.

"Do you know what forgiveness is, Ian? Maybe you need to forgive that man who did that to you."

I sensed through the Holy Spirit that Ian wanted to be freed of his pain, and I knew forgiveness would be the first step. But I didn't know how to get him to that place or what to say next.

"Okay, let's pray, then," I finally said.

"God, would you forgive the man who did these bad things to Ian? God, would You touch this young man's heart that has been trampled over by his stepfather? Father, would You show him a way to forgive and not to blame You? Most of all, I pray that he can see Your love for him."

When I opened my eyes, Ian's expression had changed. Gone was his defensive, angry street-kid look, replaced with the face of a vulnerable young man with tears filling his eyes. He no longer looked like he was refusing to feel pain. Being willing to show his pain was a huge step for Ian, I thought.

Ian and I talked a little longer. I shared how Jesus died on the cross and how Jesus could come and live in his heart. When I asked Ian if he would like to pray and ask God to take charge of his life, he eagerly nodded.

I placed my hand on Ian's back to pray, but he reached back and removed my hand.

"I'm sorry, Ian. I know your trust has been betrayed."

I started to pray, and he repeated my prayer, asking God into his heart.

"Ian," I asked, "where did you ask Christ to come?"

"Into my heart."

I could tell he had more he wanted to say. After I waited a couple of moments for Ian to speak, he finally broke the silence.

"I need to tell you something. I have been doing something really bad."

"Okay," I said. "Tell me what you have been doing."

"You see those men over there dressed as women?" He looked toward the group of transvestites I had noticed a few minutes earlier. "One of those men gives me money to have sex with him at the end of the night if he doesn't get any dates."

"How long have you been doing that?" I asked.

"Three months."

"How often?"

"About once a week."

"How much does he pay you?"

"Thirty *reais*." That was between eight and nine U.S. dollars.

I wanted to stay calm for Ian's sake, but anger was boiling up within me. Considering the cause, I like to believe it was righteous anger.

"Can you tell me which one?" I asked.

Ian looked afraid. "I am just saying this because soon he's going to ask me to do it, and I don't want to. I am afraid he might beat me up."

I wanted to proceed carefully with Ian.

"You trusted me to tell me this," I told him. "Will you trust me to resolve this situation for you?"

I reached for one of my business cards. "If he bothers you again, here is my cell phone number so you can call me."

"Okay," Ian said hesitantly.

"Ian," I said and then paused. "You really don't want to do this again, do you?"

"No," he replied.

"Then tell me which man it is."

Once Ian felt sure the transvestite wasn't watching him, he pointed the man out.

Part of our team was talking to the group of transvestites, and two of our team members were standing near the man Ian pointed to.

It was 4:15 a.m., and we had planned to leave more than an hour earlier to minister in Copacabana. But this problem had to be resolved right then and there. I walked over to a team member and asked him to pray for me, then continued over to the transvestite.

"Are you from the church?" the transvestite asked. I hadn't even reached him yet, and he hadn't turned around to face me to ask the question. "I already told those other people that I am not talking to them."

He was facing the street, and I walked around in front of him so he would have to face me. To make sure I had his full attention, I placed my big body between him and his potential customers. He stepped over to the side so he could have a line of vision to the passing cars.

I was direct and firm when I spoke. "I need to have a serious conversation with you, and it's not about Jesus."

"Are you the police?"

As calmly as I could, considering the circumstances, I replied, "It would be good for you to think that I am the police. What is your street name?"

"That's not important," he smarted back to me. Saying he needed to make a phone call, he reached for his pocketbook. I couldn't let him reach into that pocketbook because I didn't want a can of mace, a knife, or a gun winding up in my face.

He asked harshly in his falsetto woman's voice, "Do you know where I work at?"

I thought he might be threatening me, so I told him, "No, I do not know where you work, but I am not here to talk about Jesus. I am here to talk about a young boy."

When I said that, the man started squirming like a worm on a hook.

He switched to his deep, man's voice. "What, young boy?"

I motioned him over to a nearby set of tables and chairs, and we sat down.

"I need you to listen, and then you can respond," I told him. "If you have ever seen us out here before, you have seen that we minister to the street kids. Well, tonight, I learned something about you."

Without identifying Ian, I repeated what I had been told.

"If anything happens to that kid," I warned him, "I want you to know that I have two good friends, and I will call them to take care of this situation."

He could tell by my tone of voice that by "friends," I meant not-so-friendly men who wouldn't take kindly to a transvestite sexually abusing a thirteen-year-old boy.

"In fact," I said, reaching for my cell phone, "I could call them right now."

I was bluffing because I had no intention of actually placing the call. But the transvestite dropped his head onto the table. His real hair showed from beneath his wig.

"Pick your head up and look at me," I ordered him. The man did something I wasn't expecting—he admitted I was correct. He had been having a relationship with the boy, he confessed but thought that it was a mutual relationship.

"Well, he doesn't want to do that anymore," I told him, saying it clearly enough so that there could be no misunderstanding. "And I want to make sure that it doesn't happen again."

"Where do you work?" I asked him. Throughout the conversation, I had the nagging sense that he looked familiar.

"That's not important," he said. A few minutes earlier, he had wanted to use his place of employment to threaten me, but with the tables now turned, he wanted to keep his occupation secret.

His head was back down on the table by that point, but I kept looking at him, trying to figure out where I had seen him. I thought it might have been in high-profile offices in Rio where I had led devotions, but I wasn't sure. He was dressed like a woman, making it difficult to place him.

He continued to sit there, head down on the table, not volunteering any information.

"I think I need to call my friends and let them know about you," I told him.

A television van drove by us right when I said that, and when the transvestite spotted the van, he bolted from the table. With my bad knees, I knew there was no way I could chase down even a man running in high heels. If he was that afraid of the media, I thought, he had to have worked in some type of public setting or government office.

I spent the next forty-five minutes searching for Ian, but I could not find him. For the next three weeks, every time we came back to that area to minister to the street kids, I looked for Ian. Not once did I see him.

I wondered what had happened with Ian and whether the transvestite had taken my message to heart. That third week after I had confronted the transvestite, I was scheduled to lead a morning devotion for a Christian businessman's club. After that meeting, on a hunch, I stopped by the offices where I suspected the transvestite worked. I knew a Christian secretary there, and I asked if I could hang out outside her office for a while. For almost an hour, I sat in the hallway and prayed until what appeared to be a delegation of Arab businessmen walked in my direction. The voice of the local man leading the men down the hallway sounded familiar. I watched the group with interest, and when I could see the local man leading them, I recognized him as the transvestite I had confronted on Ian's behalf. Dressed in men's clothing, he looked every bit the dignified civil servant.

When the group came near, I rose from my seat but didn't say a word. That got the man's attention, and when he looked at me, he recognized me. I could almost watch the color drain from his bronzed, Brazilian skin. It took every ounce of determined effort within me not to burst out in laughter. I motioned to the man as though I wanted to have a private talk with him, even though I knew there was no way he was going to stop. He abruptly turned his face away from me and quickened the pace in leading the group past me. The visitors looked at each other with puzzled expressions.

Satisfied that the man had learned that he could run but not hide from his horrendous actions, I left city hall.

Two weeks later, I finally ran into Ian on the streets.

"Have you seen that guy who was bothering you?" I asked.

"No," he happily reported.

Not only had Ian not seen the man, but Ian also said the man had not bothered any of his friends, either, since my little sidewalk chat with him.

I continued to see Ian on the streets for the next two years, and he always seemed to be doing as well as a street kid could do. I was amazed at the transformation that took place in his life.

But when I was back in the United States for a short visit, I received heartbreaking news: Ian had been struck by random police gunfire on the streets and was killed. I still think about the spiritual innocence he showed the night when he told me, "I have been doing something really bad."

1 John 1:9 says, "If we confess our sins, He is faithful and just and will forgive us our sins and purify us from all unrighteousness" (NKJV). In addition to God forgiving us when we confess our sins, He wants us to forgive one another the same way "even as God in Christ forgave you" (Ephesians 4:32, NKJV).

We adults can find it difficult to say words like Ian's to God and to each other—to admit our sins. Ian is an example of how simple, by the grace of God, it should be to have our guilt and shame removed from us, to have our conscience cleansed by God's forgiveness.

I shed tears for my young friend when I learned he had been killed, and I thanked God for His grace that had allowed Ian to accept

Christ. I am confident that I will see my young friend again on the streets—the pure and peaceful streets of heaven.

'Righteous' Anger

I grew up in an angry environment and lived among angry people for most of my years before moving to Brazil. I suffered through stretches in my life when I didn't yield to the Holy Spirit and lost control of my anger, too.

God doesn't command us not to be angry. Matthew, Mark, Luke, and John—all four Gospels—tell us the story of Jesus using physical means to cleanse the temple upon seeing it had been turned into a den of thieves. Jesus displayed what we have come to term a "righteous anger."

The question isn't whether we will have anger. We will. The question is, what will we do with our anger?

When angered, we face the temptation to do things in our own strength or use the world's ways instead of relying on the Lord. I confess that I used boldness and intimidation to scare the transvestite into staying away from Ian. But I remember that the apostle Paul used his status as a Roman citizen to put the fear of Rome into the commander who was about to punish him unlawfully, and it worked for Paul.[iv]

I put the fear of a couple of thugs I knew (and, hopefully, the fear of God) into the transvestite abusing Ian, and it worked. It was a fine line, but it was one worth walking as long as we stayed on the correct side.

And that's why we needed to make sure we keep the Holy Spirit in the picture. Under the Holy Spirit's guidance, anger is a good thing. It can motivate us. It can stir up our passions. It can get us off our backsides and into action.

Our anger was a major reason our team reached out to the street kids.

When we saw the kids—and, as I've said, there were thousands of them—we could not tell why or how they got there. But we did know that deep down, they all wished they were safe and warm, tucked snugly into beds like the rest of Rio's children.

As the father of two daughters, it was inconceivable that my girls would be forced to live homeless, on the streets, without protection. The thought was nauseating.

Not only were kids out there, but they also were considered a menace, or like "wild horses," as the one woman said. That angered me, and the Holy Spirit took my anger and motivated me to do something about it.

Our ministry team would not sit by and make those children have to fend for themselves.

From Ramona's prayer journal:

"Lord, you said that we could be angry but sin not. So, we are angry, Lord, about the situations these kids have here in Rio on the streets. We know that it is Your desire that all men be saved. Lord, let these little children come unto You in the way in which You see fit. May the family, Reese, and the team be used in ways in which You see fit to love on these kids weekly or monthly, as opportunities are given. Lord, protect these kids, keep them from hurt, harm, or danger. In Jesus' name, I pray."

Chapter 14

Love to Lead, Lead to Love

I am a leader. I don't hesitate to describe myself that way.

Other people also call me a leader. Sometimes it's because they know I have a title. Sometimes it's because they know I lead ministry teams. Sometimes, they don't know anything about me, but they determine I must be a leader when I get up in front of people and talk with a loud voice. As if that truly qualifies for me anything other than being loud.

Here, though, is the reason why I call myself a leader: I'm alive and breathing.

The truth is that everybody leads or can lead. It doesn't require having a title or responsibility or some kind of recognition from others. All it takes is a need and a willingness to serve regardless of the cost.

Books on leadership line bookstore shelves. Search for podcasts on leadership, and the options seem endless. Leadership is a favorite subject of mine. I've read many books on the topic, and I took leadership classes in seminary, where we studied Jesus' leadership. I've also observed missionaries, both the ones whom I consider successful and those who admit they are or appear to be at a standstill in their ministry.

From that database of knowledge, I began to apply principles that I believed would work for our ministry in Brazil. I noticed that being a missionary tends to force a person to step up to the plate and make choices and decisions. I know I haven't had the highest batting average on the mission field. Sometimes I've struck out, and sometimes I've hit a home run. But along the way, I've developed a list of six leadership principles that have been successful in Brazil and, I believe, will work in most places.

1. Work as part of a team.

Ramona and I are in Brazil at the request of the Brazilian Baptist Convention. Therefore, we work *with them* to reach people for Christ. Working with others doesn't mean you always agree with them. There will be times when we disagree about the methods used in reaching people for Christ, but they always will be agreeable disagreements. We will not have disagreements over major theological issues because we both believe that people need Christ.

2. Seek advice.

I am not an expert on missions in Brazil. I don't know all the answers. In fact, I probably have more questions than answers. I also am not the owner of all truth. That is why I consult with the Brazilian national pastors for advice. I also seek advice from American pastors for whom I have much respect. I ask for guidance from experienced missionaries and leaders with the Southern Baptist Convention. I ask questions of my brethren from other denominations who have the same calling here in Brazil. A leader never stops learning, and one of the best ways to keep learning is to be willing to learn from others.

3. Be transparent.

I tend to be very open and honest about my personal life, my vision, my hurts, and my disappointments. Some people don't understand why I am so open. One of our short-term summer volunteers commented during an evaluation that I was compassionate and transparent yet added that I was so transparent it made her uncomfortable. I asked her to explain. She told me, "You expose your heart so easily to those on your team that there are times when they might see you as weak." I responded by explaining, "Oh, no, the Bible says that when we are weak, He is strong." I am weak, and I can do nothing without His strength, and I don't try to hide that. In fact, I want everyone to see that I have weaknesses so that all glory can be rightly given to God.

4. Be on the same level as others.

Jesus is fully deity, yet He came to our level as humans in order to lead us back into a relationship with the Father. A person who gets a big head is headed for a big fall. My favorite expression is, "Everyone has the same value at the foot of the cross." It is another way of saying the ground is level at the foot of the cross. Pride is the most common sin in ministry. I pray that Jesus helps me not become filled with pride. Jesus loved other people, He never put Himself above other people, and He told us to love our neighbor as we love ourselves. We cannot love someone as we love ourselves if we have placed ourselves on a level above theirs. I don't consider Brazilians to be *those* people; they are *my* people. If I ever try to place myself on a higher level because I am an American or a missionary, I'm done for here and might as well pack up the family and head back to Georgia.

5. Lead people to Jesus.

That sounds obvious, but leading people to Jesus must be one of the most important principles of being a leader in ministry. I'll share later about overcoming my inability to say no, but that is an answer I give when asked to do good things that do not have leading people to Christ as their either their direct or indirect purpose. If I'm not careful, I can allow good projects to become an obstacle to the greater goal. I wholeheartedly support good things that others are doing and do not want to come across as possessing a trace of spiritual snobbery, but my job is to obey God's specific calling for me to preach the gospel and lead people to Christ. My calling might be different than the next person's. All my time and resources are allocated to obeying *my* calling, even at the expense of things that are "good."

6. Live a balanced life.

This is one of the most difficult principles for leaders to maintain, yet it also is one of the most important. Family, ministry, health, and personal devotion to God must be kept in balance. All it takes to throw things out of balance is for one area to be off. One of the more common causes for an imbalance that I've seen in the ministry is leaders who become full of themselves. When their focus is on themselves, they lose sight of the importance of maintaining balance, and constant monitoring and evaluation are required to keep that balance. I once posed this question to a group of pastors: "Do you have any trouble taking time off from ministry to take your wife out to dinner?" I only asked because I had struggled big-time in that area. Most of the pastors told me that spending the proper amount of time with their families was one of their greater challenges in the ministry.

The common thread that must run through these six principles is love.

Love is what has allowed me to be accepted working in a different culture than my own. One difference I have noticed between the Brazilian church and the American church is the emphasis on relationships. In the United States, there can be too much emphasis placed on a church's building and a church's programs. In Brazil, where the buildings don't offer much, and the programs barely exist, the gospel has spread because of relationships. It's me loving someone enough to share the gospel with him, and then he, in turn, loving someone else enough to share the gospel with that person.

I confess that it was often difficult for me to like some of the drug dealers or the transvestites when I first started ministering here in Brazil. But it didn't take me long after sitting on a large rock and talking with a drug dealer to realize that, first and foremost, he was a human being who needed Jesus. And it didn't take me long to learn that all the transvestites and prostitutes really wanted was someone to care for them. In those regards, the drug dealers and the transvestites, and the prostitutes are no different than I had once been.

Except for the grace of God, we all are lost.

God's Standard: Faithfulness

Outside of those principles, there are three other observations about leadership that I like to share.

First, a leader can't ask people to go where he doesn't go. A leader cannot lead people to a place where he has not first been himself.

Second, a person's ability to lead often is best reflected when he's *not* there. If a leader leaves and things fall apart in his absence, he most likely wasn't leading well while present. My leadership strategy is not developed for while I am here, but for when I'm not here—either when I'm back in the States for a time or for if God calls us to be elsewhere. I evaluate my leadership in Rio, for example, based on the times I was not there. If I had trained my team members well when I wasn't there, they still were able to see and evaluate situations and then identify solutions.

Third, we tend to focus too much on results. More specifically, we tend to err by focusing too much on what *we* think the results should be. Yes, there must be results that accompany leadership, but there are different types of results[v], and no two leaders' results will be the same.

A discouraged colleague once talked with me about his ministry with a creative-access group. Those are people who live in countries where traditional missionaries are not allowed. Although they are most commonly called restricted-access people or countries, we know they are not to be ignored, so we refer to them in the positive manner of *creative*-access people.

My friend wasn't seeing the results from his ministry that he believed he should be seeing. He said that when he compared his ministry's results with the results of our ministry in Brazil, he considered himself a failure.

Hearing him say that broke my heart.

Comparisons, especially in ministry, rarely are accurate barometers for success because comparisons reflect *our* standards for results, not God's.

I told my colleague, "Comparing my ministry to your ministry is not a good thing because missionaries in places like yours will love the people, work hard, and ask God to reveal ways to bring people to the Lord, but still see little fruit from their efforts. There are missionaries in other settings who can walk down the street and say, 'Jesus is Lord' and flocks will come to know Christ. You are faced with more difficult circumstances. You can't compare your ministry with another's ministry."

He was ready to quit the ministry, and I didn't want that. God knows that I have battled discouragement, too, and even wanted to quit, and go home on a couple of occasions.

My advice to my friend was this: "Decide now that when times of discouragement come, you will continue to serve God rather than returning home. You were not called by the people you minister to—you were called by God. So, determine that whatever happens, you will persevere."

I reminded my friend about the Old Testament prophet Jeremiah, who saw little fruit and was even thrown into prison by the high priest. But the Bible calls Jeremiah faithful to the end.

The true measure of leadership in God's sight is not results—it's faithfulness.

From Ramona's prayer journal:
"Lord, teach my husband to lead like Jesus. May our team be servant-leaders. Make us all servant leaders Lord, so that others may come to You."

Chapter 15

'No' Is My Friend

"You're not Jesus."

My wife had to occasionally remind me of that because I experienced times in Rio when I became overwhelmed by the needs there.

When that happened, I prayed. Then I talked to Ramona, and she helped me see my frailty, what we could realistically do there, and what we could not do. That was when she'd remind me that I wasn't Jesus.

I've always been a fix-it guy. I'm not a "mechanical-type fix-it guy," but someone who feels the need to make everything better for everyone. As a kid, I wanted to make things better for Momma even though there was little I could do at that age. In college, I started the Black Men in Unity group because I wanted to fix the problem of young black men growing up without fathers to mentor them and to teach them how to live. In the military, my can-do spirit earned me promotions.

I was the type of person who had a habit of seeing things that weren't like they should be and assumed it was my job to set them right. Many times, frankly, I succeeded. Sometimes, I didn't. But to me, it was more important I at least try, whether or not I succeeded.

The way that I'm wired, my solution to problems is to work even harder. That's a dangerous solution—not the same "dangerous" that could cost me my life in Rio, but the type of danger that could cost me the life that God wants me to lead. I would much rather die living out my calling than live a long time not living the life God designed for me.

We ministered in eighteen favelas, and we could have worked on only one mountainside until we died and made a drop of a difference in relation to the overall need.

I got overwhelmed thinking, *I've got to do this, I've got to do this, and I've got to do this.*

Rio had more "this" than I can handle, and Ramona was good about making sure I remembered that.

In Matthew 6, when a woman poured out her alabaster flask filled with expensive, fragrant oil, the disciples became indignant—there's that word again—because they believed the oil had been wasted. In their minds, the oil would have been better served by being sold and the money given to the poor. Jesus came to the woman's defense because she had appropriately focused on Jesus as His time on earth was beginning to wind down. "For you have the poor with you always, but Me you do not always have."

Ramona reminded me of Jesus's words on multiple occasions when I took on the disciples' mindset and acted as though I could best serve by placing my focus more on the poor of Rio than on Jesus Himself.

The first time Ramona told me, "the poor we'll always have with us," I got offended. Seriously, I was offended.

"What do you mean we'll have the poor with us?" I responded to her in my loud, worked-up voice. "We're called to be missionaries to help the people here. And because we'll have the poor always, does that mean I don't give them everything I've got?"

To answer my own question, I was not to give the poor everything I had; I was to give Christ everything I had.

Learning that lesson was a humbling experience.

Saving a Marriage

Looking back, I see two areas in which I was slower than I should have been in making the transition from an unmarried, still-maturing Christian to a husband, father, and more spiritually mature missionary.

First, I knew in my heart that I needed to depend less on my strengths and abilities and rely more on God and the spiritual gifts He had given me. My heart knew it, but my mind was slower to grasp that. I can't pinpoint a light-switch moment where I can say, "That's when it started," but I do see that it took me several years into our time in Brazil to come to understand the importance of being submitted fully to God's strength and His gifts. And I would not dare say I mastered that. Far from it. Every Christian must learn this, and even when we can claim that we've learned it, it's another matter when it comes to putting that lesson into practice. It's a perpetual battle to get out of that "I've gotta do this" mindset.

Second, as a husband and father, it took me a while to realize that living as "we" is much, much different than living as "me." The fallout from overextending myself carries ramifications for more than me because my choices and actions have *direct* implications on my family.

My save-the-world mentality did not work well for my family, and it took time for me to see I was short-changing my wife and daughters. By trying to give everything I had to minister in the *favelas*, I was robbing Ramona and the girls of having my best in terms of time and attention.

I know that's a common problem in the ministry. Not to make an excuse but to highlight the problem; it's easy to see the overwhelming need and think, *the people need me*. It's easy to assume the need presents the call, that because we see a need, we are the ones who must take care of it. Experience taught me that's an extremely deceptive form of pride because I had the attitude that my strengths and abilities were going to waste if I wasn't trying to meet every need in the *favelas*.

The truth is, a minister can keep thinking *the people need me* until the people who need him most, those God has called him to reach most—his family—can say, "See ya'." But for the grace of God, I might have become one of those ministers who gave everything he had to his ministry at the expense of his marriage and family.

The first thing I had to learn was how to say no. Ramona knew how to say no, but she shares now how she had to learn to use it more. But that word wasn't in my vocabulary.

With my obsession for working in Rio and Ramona's heart of gold, we were like one candle burning at both ends. It was my fault we allowed that to happen. If I had been wise enough to realize the potential destruction we were flirting with bringing into our marriage, I know that Ramona would have agreed with me that we needed to change our priorities. It was up to me to be responsible and to lead in our marriage, but I missed the danger signs. Fortunately, some of the leaders in my missions agency loved Ramona and me enough to step in and do something about it.

I'm sure it is difficult to pull someone off the mission field, but that's what our leaders did. They brought us back to the States for two months so we could undergo counseling on how to maintain balance and priorities in our lives. I am grateful for their boldness because it likely saved our marriage and ministry.

Being called on the carpet by the agency leaders was a humbling experience. They made me realize, for the first time that I could remember as a Christian, that God is God, and I am not. I was not intentionally trying to play God, but it appeared that way.

I was trying to meet every need and solve every problem in the *favelas*, but I had to acknowledge that I could help only a small fraction of the people. I had to admit to myself that God hadn't sent me to the *favelas* to save the *favelas*. Instead, he had sent me, above all else, to be faithful to Him. And that meant taking care of Ramona and the girls first and foremost.

We had a team of people working in the *favelas* to meet the needs that the poor could not meet on their own. But Ramona, Gloria, and Alicia had needs that no one but I could meet. If I failed to meet my wife's and daughters' needs, then I would be guilty of being out of God's will more than if I failed to meet every need in the slums.

During our counseling sessions, I learned that one of our first mistakes after arriving in Brazil was not scheduling regular family time. Being flexible was important to us. "Flexible" can be a ministry word for justifying work gluttony. With no times set aside for our family, ministry dominated our schedule.

With guidance, Ramona and I laid out a schedule that the family would follow. We determined when we would have family times, when I would conduct ministry in the slums and the streets, how often we would take a weekend getaway as a family or a couple, who would oversee our family and ministry budgets, and who would comprise our ministry staff. We also set guidelines for when and how to say no to outside requests for help that could impact our lives in significant ways. We then agreed to review all those areas every three months to evaluate how we were doing and make any necessary adjustments.

We still maintained a busy schedule, that's for sure. A "routine" week for me looked like this:

Sunday: This day reflected an adjustment we made. Sunday was a busy ministry day from morning until late at night because I accepted invitations to speak in churches for morning and evening services. One of our adjustments was me rarely guest speaking on Sunday mornings. Our family attended a church in the city rather than a *favela* church because I believed it important for my wife and kids to be fed spiritually. If we attend a *favela* church, they would have been asked to help, and we wanted our girls, especially, to be ministered to regularly. Plus, being plain old, run-of-the-mill churchgoers allowed Gloria and Alicia to be ordinary kids. When I agreed to speak on a Sunday, it was almost exclusively for an evening service.

Monday: This was my day to rest and make specific plans for the upcoming week with Ramona.

Tuesday: I conducted church training, performed visitation in the slums, and prepared for the all-nighter that was our "Care Night" street ministry.

Wednesday: I slept in after Care Night, did more church training (especially at mid-weeknight services), and visited people in the slums.

Thursday: Ramona and I meet for brunch, lunch, or coffee while the girls were in school. I spent the late afternoon and evening at home with my family before our second "Care Night" of the week.

Friday: I often didn't return home from Care Night until dawn, so I slept in before catching up on office work. Friday night was our family night!

Saturday: Every other Saturday was a team ministry in a community. I reserved the other Saturdays for relaxing and hanging out as a family.

Every day, Ramona and I set aside alone time with the Lord and for studying His Word. We also spent time in the gym to maintain our physical health. Every night, Ramona and I tried to spend an hour together, talking about anything and everything related to our personal and family lives. I had to spend time with the Lord, and I had to spend time with my wife. If either of those was lacking, it would cause great problems.

Before counseling helped us come up with that schedule, my planner would have read something like this:

Days beginning with a capital letter and ending in 'y': Ministry.

My secretary was a big help in keeping me on schedule. Monday was my off day, and that had been a day when I forsook the rest my body's needed to go do more of "the people need me" ministry. She took all my calls on Monday and made sure none of the non-emergency items made it to me on that day. She handled any appointment-making that came on a Monday. And because our office received so many requests for help—and worthy requests in most cases, such as helping an American church raise money for a needed building—she also possessed full authority to turn down requests that she knew fell outside of the area we felt our ministry was called by God to do.

It wasn't that I didn't want to help in those ways, but I had already experienced what happened when I took on too many things that weren't in the middle of that God-calling zone our ministry had. Having someone like my secretary, who I was able to be on the page some with, was invaluable to keeping to the schedule Ramona and I set up and knew we must adhere to.

Our marriage and our ministry benefited immensely from the action plans developed during counseling. Having a regular schedule built for our family and for the Lord made a noticeable impact on our marriage.

Even though our desire to be flexible was part of our problem, we noticed the schedule we arranged actually allowed for flexibility. Funny how that worked. And, of course, there were emergencies that came up. So, our schedule did not become a rut that bogged us down. Instead, establishing our family time as a priority became a foundation on which we built all our ministry tasks.

Besides, we realized that we were justifying being "flexible" by our love for people and the Lord when we had actually come to love service more than the people. And we did love the people. That tells you how into service we were. Service had become our idol, and I took great delight—even pride, I'll admit—in being "the man with the plan."

From my experience and from talking with missionaries in different parts of the world, when poor people in other cultures learn we are from America, they think we can take care of all of, or at least many of, their problems. And most aren't shy about asking for help. That's no blame on them; that's human nature.

During our early years in Rio, we received phone calls at all hours of the night from people asking for help. Ramona struggled to say no, and most of the time, I just flat out didn't say it. Had to meet the needs, you know.

Our counseling sessions in the States provided us with a tool that changed our lives. The "RAC" method keys on three words:

- Responsible: Who will be responsible?
- Approval: Who holds the final approval?
- Consult: Did you consult the other person?

I began asking the three RAC questions when making big decisions, and that helped diminish my impulsiveness and increased our communication as a couple.

'RAC' in Action

Here is how we put the RAC method into action: First, we decided together which one of us would be *responsible* for the area of activity. Second, one of us was designated to determine whether to give final *approval* to our involvement in the action. Third, we vowed to *consult* with each other throughout the process.

A situation that illustrates how the RAC method played out involved a single mother named Lucy.

Lucy had found herself in abusive relationships time after time, but Ramona led her to Christ and was discipling her through Bible study. Lucy constantly depended on us to help her, and she was quite needy. Saying no to her was difficult for both of us because of the dramatic transformation we observed in her life.

In the middle of the night, we received a call from Lucy. She needed someone to take her child to the hospital in a non-life-threatening situation. To help Lucy would have required that both of us take her and her child to the hospital. Me going along with Lucy would have been inappropriate, and it would have been too dangerous for Ramona to be out with Lucy that late at night. Both of us taking Lucy, however, meant leaving our daughters home alone in the middle of the night, and that wasn't an option.

Ramona had developed a close relationship with Lucy through her ministry, so because I had a less emotional attachment to the request, we decided I would take responsibility for assessing the situation. Because of the reasons already mentioned, I did not believe I should approve of answering Lucy's request to take her to the hospital. I explained why I felt that way to Ramona—I consulted with her—and she agreed we could not take Lucy and her child to the hospital. Because of Ramona's relationship with Lucy, I called Lucy and told her we could not take her. I suggested she call a taxi or wait until morning.

Another night, the representative of a local community official called and asked that I come quickly to mediate a dispute between drug dealers and police. The two sides had been squaring off in shootouts for two weeks, and innocent people had been killed by crossfire. The community had been brought to a standstill, with schools and stores shutting down.

What had been a bad-enough situation escalated when police shot and killed a drug dealer after he surrendered. Following that incident, another drug dealer, who also had surrendered, escaped, and reported the killing to the top drug lord. The drug lord responded by ordering his forces to block the community streets to prevent any traffic.

Cars and buses were burned, stores were looted, and innocent people were killed. Violence then spread from that community to other communities. The media devoted a lot of coverage to what was going on, and I had been closely following the stories.

For mountainside *favelas* dominated by drug factions, the drug lord occupies the highest part of the mountain. Elite soldiers had been brought in to move up the mountain to take over the drug lord's stronghold, but they couldn't make much progress up the mountain because the drug faction had blocked the street with burned cars. Tractors were brought in to remove the cars, but one of the tractor drivers was shot in the shoulder. The drug lord's men also poured oil onto the streets so that armored police cars would spin out and be halted from moving up toward the place from where the drug lord was directing the resistance.

That was when I received the phone call asking for my assistance. The escaped drug dealer had sent a message to police requesting that I mediate his re-surrender. I guess he hoped that having the American missionary as mediator would help him avoid the same fate as the other dealer who had been shot dead by police.

I told the representative that I would call him back in a few minutes. Ramona was in the room with me when I fielded the call, and I filled her in on the request. We agreed I should call my missions supervisor.

"How are you going to go up the mountainside?" he asked. "What safety is guaranteed to you?"

I explained that the police would take me up the mountain in an armored vehicle, and I would escort the escaped drug dealer back down the mountain so he could make a statement and turn himself in.

My supervisor didn't say anything for a moment. Then he asked one more question.

"What does Ramona think?"

Ramona was near enough to me that she heard the supervisor's question. I handed her the phone, and she began talking with him. Ramona and my supervisor agreed that my putting myself into the situation could be harmful to our ministry and that there were too many unknowns and not enough guarantees of a peaceful outcome.

Ramona took responsibility for the decision because I was too emotionally involved with the situation. She told me why she could not approve of my involvement. She consulted with me, and forty-five minutes after the request came in, I called back and declined the invitation. I did tell them, however, that I would be willing to consider other opportunities to help in the future. I didn't want to close down the line of communication that had been opened.

What does Ramona think?

Considering that question represented another way in which God has helped me shift my thinking over time. Growing up in the poor, black South, I didn't see women always treated with respect, must less as equal to men.

Ramona is a strong woman who deserves and commands respect. Through our marriage counseling, I learned that I needed to go beyond being nice and respectful to her. In 1 Peter 3:7, husbands are admonished to dwell with their wives "with understanding, giving honor to the wife, as to the weaker vessel [with "weaker" referring to physical strength], and as being heirs together of the grace of life, that your prayers may not be hindered" (NKJV).

The modern-day Eric Reese interpretation of that verse is that "what Ramona thinks" is every bit as important as what Reese thinks. I think that I had always believed that, but Ramona came to believe that I believed it. (When I read the story in Matthew 27 of Jesus being sentenced to crucify, I imagine that Pontius Pilate wished he had listened more to his wife's thoughts.)

With the mediation request I wound up declining, the temptation to accept came from concern over a missed opportunity—not necessarily the present opportunity, but future chances to minister that might come out of saying yes to this request.

I learned a lesson there, too, because a week later, the same official's office called again, asking if our team would set up our tent at the entrance to the community and offer a week-long health and hygiene clinic. The official said his office would supply doctors for the week and allow us to hold worship services at night. This community had been through all kinds of turmoil and needed the help I knew our ministry could provide.

I don't know if I could have asked for a better deal if I had tried to negotiate one over the phone back on that first night his office had called. It sounded too good to be true. We all know what that means—it *was* too good to be true.

In talking with people in that community, I discovered the authorities had wanted our ministry to help in such a visible manner so the official would look good to the media after all the violence that had taken place there. Basically, they wanted to use our ministry to create good publicity for themselves.

When his office called to follow up on the offer, I said no. For our team members' safety, we pulled out of ministry altogether in that community until things quieted down.

Before our counseling and learning to use the RAC method, I likely would have impulsively said yes to all three of those situations—Lucy, who needed a middle-of-the-night ride to the hospital for her child that wasn't an emergency, putting my life at risk by mediating between the drug dealer and the police, and exposing our team members to possible jeopardy in a dangerous environment. One irresponsible, selfish decision could have left me picking up the pieces of tragedy.

In working my way through this issue, I became curious about how Jesus knew when to say yes and when to say no. I haven't come up with my final answer yet, but I did find an insightful chain of verses in the fifth chapter of John that provides some clues. Consider a couple of those verses:

Verse 19: "Then Jesus answered and said to them, 'Most assuredly, I say to you, the Son can do nothing of Himself, but what He sees the Father do; for whatever He does, the Son also does in like manner" (NKJV).

And verse 30: "I can of Myself do nothing. As I hear, I judge; and My judgment is righteous because I do not seek My own will but the will of the Father who sent Me" (NKJV).

It seems like Jesus was always asking, "What would the Father do in this situation?" I might not be able to answer that question as Jesus could, but based on His example, it does appear to be a great place to start.[vi]

Ramona and I—especially me—continued to learn how to say no when that was the proper answer. We make sure we arrived at that answer together, just as we arrived at a yes answer together.

There were a lot of things we couldn't do. But there were also many things we would *not* do. Saying no was gut-wrenching sometimes, considering my natural desire to fix anyone's problems regardless of the potential cost.

Ramona knew when I need help in this area. When I got tired, and that led to physical ailments, Ramona stepped in and told my secretary, "My husband isn't doing anything else until he gets rested."

So, it was not only me who understood the importance of my understanding I'm not Jesus.

That accomplish-all-things attitude that once could have been my downfall became my best weapon in defending my relationship with my family. That's because having a family that honored the Lord became my number one goal and priority.

No longer was saying yes always the best way to accomplish my goals. Due to my new top goal and priority, I learned that saying no is often the best way.

From Ramona's prayer journal:
"Lord, make us one. Our marriage is your affair. May it reflect You."

Eric Reese

Chapter 16

Leave or Stay?

Ramona was crying when she called, her voice shaking.

"Someone just called and said that my husband is going to be filled with bullets!"

I returned directly home. She was still sobbing when I walked in the door, and when I saw how frightened she was, I reacted poorly.

Death threats were serious business in the *favelas*. Mine came as the result of something good our ministry was doing in Castle City. Our free health and hygiene clinics had been well received in various communities and also had served as a point of entry for our ministry in some of those communities. We decided to go a step further in Castle City and set up a salon offering our same health and hygiene services and also offer haircuts at a minimal cost. The salon would serve as a permanent place in the community where we could talk with residents about the gospel and distribute spiritual literature.

In our planning, though, we hadn't considered our salon could lead to a death threat.

Castle City was controlled by a paramilitary group, and Jack, one of the top leaders, signed off on us opening a salon. As a public show of support for our presence, Jack had his hair cut there and made himself a regular at our salon. That brought us instant credibility. Jack and I also began developing a friendship through his visits.

Another paramilitary official also owned a hair salon there, and he didn't like competition for his business.

A few weeks after our opening, I was standing outside the salon when Jack walked up and asked how things were going. I told him I was on the fence about whether we should keep the salon open. The health services part was going well, but I was disappointed in the limited opportunities we'd had to share the gospel in the salon. I explained sharing the gospel was our most important reason for opening the place because we wanted to help people spiritually as well as with their physical needs. I told Jack I wasn't sure if we were accomplishing our spiritual goal.

"I think you are, Pastor," Jack said. His answer surprised me because we had yet to have a serious talk about the gospel. I considered his response an opening to present the gospel to the most powerful man in the area.

"Where do you attend church?" I asked.

"I haven't been to church in years," he replied.

"Have you ever heard of Jesus?" I asked.

"Sure," Jack said. "Jesus Christ."

"Did you ever hear that Christ—"

"Died on the cross?" Jack interrupted. "Yeah, sure. Let me stop you right there. My ex-wife is in church every Sunday, and I admire her for her faith. But I want to be honest with you. I am doing things now that I don't think will allow me to go to church. God wouldn't accept those things."

"I really appreciate that you don't want to be a hypocrite," I said, "but the Bible says in Romans 5:20 that where sin multiplied, grace multiplied even more. I don't know what bad things you are doing, but it's incorrect to think we can't go to church if we sin. Christ accepts us coming to Him just the way we are. We don't get fixed up to go to Christ; we go to Christ to get fixed up."

"Pastor, let me make this clearer," Jack said. "The Bible says, 'Thou shalt not kill.' I have killed, and I might have to kill some more."

I appreciated his honesty.

"The Bible also says that we all have sinned and fall short of the glory of God," I explained. "There is no big or little sin. It's all sin."

"Well, I don't think you can compare killing to someone who simply didn't tell the truth."

"In your mind, you think killing is worse than lying," I told him. "But actually, the Bible simply speaks of sin as sin. I believe that Christ wants to come into your heart."

I intentionally was being direct with Jack. Although I felt that was the best way to witness to him, I also hoped that he wouldn't be offended. Instead, he seemed to appreciate the direct approach.

"So, you want me to put Christ in my heart?" he asked.

"Well, you don't put Him there. You invite Him to come in."

Jack chuckled, patted me on the back, and walked away. I watched him walk. He was shaking his head, and I read that as a positive sign.

Over the next three months, Jack and I continued to talk about sin, God's will, and morality. In my desire to prevent any perception of choosing sides, I didn't get close to authorities in communities—especially someone with Jack's position and power. But Jack was open to our discussions, and he was helping support our salon. On top of that, I really liked Jack.

Death Threat

The caller had told Ramona that he was an employee at the other salon in Castle City and that he was relaying a message from the owner's militia group. A trainee in our salon had gotten into an argument with an employee of the other salon, and when the owner became involved, the death threat followed.

I became so mad when I saw how frightened Ramona was that I called for a motorcycle taxi to pick me up at our house. I didn't appreciate the other salon owner upsetting my wife, and I wanted to tell him that face-to-face.

Castle City was a short trip from our home, and when we entered the community, the vice president of the community association stopped the motorcycle taxi. I knew the vice president, and when he saw how upset I was, he asked what was wrong. I told him. He immediately directed the motorcycle driver to turn around and take me straight home. Then, he instructed him to stand at my front door and not allow me to leave the house.

The driver took me back out of Castle City, and by the time we arrived home, Ramona had called our salon to alert the employees to the death threat. She had also e-mailed all our prayer intercessors and asked them to pray. Meanwhile, the news had reached Jack, and he had gone to our salon to see what he could do to help there.

An hour and a half later, I looked outside. The motorcycle taxi driver was still standing guard at the door. Being practically locked inside my own house made me almost as mad as when I had seen Ramona so upset. I opened the door and told the driver he could leave because I was going to stay inside my home like a good little boy. He looked into my eyes and said only, "Sheesh!" I guess he didn't believe me.

Half an hour later, Jack called to tell me he was taking care of the problem. "Don't worry, Pastor. Many people know the good you are doing in our community."

I explained that I wasn't worried so much about the death threat as much as I was angry that Ramona had been upset. Jack offered to talk to Ramona. I thanked him for his concern for her but told him there was no need.

A couple of hours after Jack's call, the top militia commander of Castle City called.

"Pastor Eric, Jack told me about the threat on your life. I want you to know that I have noticed your ministry and have seen how you help people. I even overheard a lady tell someone how she needed medicine for her baby, and you took her to a pharmacy to get it. We have a lot of pastors on television, but they are robbers and clowns. I detest them. But you are the first person I know who walks like he talks. I have dispatched men to talk with this man who has threatened your life and believe me; I will resolve the problem."

Tears flowed from my eyes before the commander had finished speaking. I had been through a vast range of emotions in just a few hours, beginning with the stress of a death threat and the anger of seeing my wife frightened, and now God had used a non-Christian community leader to guarantee my safety and a top paramilitary commander had affirmed our ministry team's efforts.

I thanked the commander and clicked off the call. I didn't want Ramona to see me crying, so I turned toward the window. The taxi driver—my guard—took a call on his cell phone, started up his motorcycle, and departed.

Finally, it seemed like the long ordeal had ended.

For the first time since Ramona told me of the death threat, we had a chance to sit down and talk. She had been through many different emotions, too, but now she was simply mad—mad at the man who had threatened me, mad at us having a salon in Castle City, and mad at us even working in such a dangerous community. She said if it were up to her, she would close the salon and not work again in Castle City.

I let her release her emotions. While she was talking, I listened to see if she would say what would have been the most telling statement of all: "I want to go home. I can't handle Brazil any longer."

Ramona didn't say she wanted to go home.

But I was thinking about it. I was ready to call it quits and go back to the States.

After Ramona and I finished our conversation, I made a phone call.

Stephen Kendrick was a senior associate pastor at our home church, Sherwood Baptist. More important, he's a close friend and brother in the Lord. Sherwood's pastor, Michael Catt, had told me a few times that if Ramona and I left the mission field and returned to Albany, I could work as a member of his pastoral staff.

I called Stephen to let him know I was interested in coming back to work at Sherwood. I started describing for Stephen how hurt I was, and he listened with a sympathetic heart. Then he prayed for me and confidently assured me, "God's got your back, and so does your church!"

I hung up without expressing my reason for making the call. Then I retreated to my chair.

"My chair" was an office chair in our bedroom. We didn't have a large house, so I could not have a man cave. Instead, I maintained an "office" in a corner of our bedroom. I had a small, wooden desk that a friend made for me. Actually, my desk was more like a wooden shelf attached to the wall about hip high, along with a small bookcase for my books. And then there was my chair.

I did my serious thinking and meditation in my chair. It was my little space of solitude. Ramona and the girls knew what was taking place when I was sitting in my chair and not working at my desk. Sometimes, they brought me a glass of water to sip on or even food if I had been there for a while. But they knew my chair time was not a good time to be asking Daddy a lot of questions. And Ramona knew it was a great time to pray for me.

"God, I don't understand," I angrily said. "This doesn't make any sense to me. I'm here at Your call, and I've got people threatening my life. My family. My wife. What is going on? Any $50,000-a-year job in the States is looking real good right now. I'm tired of this. I tried. But you can't go where people don't want you to go. And you can't do what people don't want you to do."

When I went to my chair, I stayed there until the issue was resolved. I stayed in my chair for eight hours, pouring out my heart to God—and, admittedly, giving Him a piece of my mind a time or two.

But the more I sat there, occasionally spinning slowly in the chair, the more I reflected on how many times I had been in dangerous situations, and God had protected me. Not only in Rio but also in Albany, in Atlanta, and in the army, God had secured me and brought me through trying circumstances. I thought of Hebrews 13:5, where God says, "I will never leave you nor forsake you." In the following verse, the writer of Hebrews writes, "So we may boldly say: 'The Lord is my helper; I will not fear. What can man to do me?'"

After hours of mentally wrestling with my calling and my circumstances, I felt comfort begin to confront the pressure that I was feeling. When comfort had won out, I stood from my chair—issue resolved—and went downstairs. Ramona was preparing food to bring up to me, and when I walked into the kitchen, she said, "Oh, praise God! He's out of his chair!"

I wasn't downstairs long, though, because I resolutely walked out the front door and headed toward the neighborhood that was home to the man who had threatened my life. I had thought of how Gideon had not been confident when he heard God's voice and had asked God multiple times to prove Himself to Gideon.

I told God. "You don't need to prove anything to me. I'm going to step out by faith into that community."

I prayer-walked through that neighborhood for an hour.

The next morning, my missionary supervisor, Nolan Pridemore, called. He had received Ramona's e-mail to our prayer intercessors. I detailed the whole story and told him there was no longer a death threat. He pledged his support for whatever we decided to do.

Then Jack called. He wanted to know if the commander had called. He reassured me the commander would stand by his word and that I no longer needed to worry about the death threat.

I didn't see Jack for another three weeks. Satisfied the situation had calmed, I returned to Castle City and bumped into Jack. He slapped me on the back as soon as I was within reaching distance.

"Put Jesus in your heart!" he told me with a big smile. He was acting like he had done the same thing himself. We both were on our way to different places, and I didn't have time to ask Jack whether he had given his life to Christ. But he seemed to be carrying the peace that only comes from Jesus.

Murder of a Friend

"Reese, where are you?"

I told Ramona I had left a meeting and was in my truck.

"Come straight home," she told me. She didn't give me any details. Only, "Come straight home."

My cell phone rang again. It was a trainee at the salon.

"Go straight home," she said. "Don't come by the salon. Just go straight home."

Sweat was beading up on the top of my head. I could feel my blood pressure rising. I pulled into a gas station to collect my thoughts.

Another salon trainee called.

"Pastor Eric, are you parked?"

"Yes, I'm sitting in my truck."

"Pastor Eric, your friend Jack has been shot eighteen times. He just died, and because you are a good friend of his, everyone is telling me to call you and tell you to stay away from here."

I was shocked.

"Who killed him?" I asked.

"I don't know," the trainee said. Then he explained that in the past, when a community authority had been killed, often friends of that authority also wound up dead.

"Please stay away," she said. "Don't come into Castle City."

I sat in my truck, unsure what to think or to do next. The gas station attendant came over and asked if I was okay.

"Can I get a cup of water?" I asked.

The attendant returned with water.

"Do you need me to take you to the hospital?" he asked.

"No, I'm okay."

I started digging around inside my bag in the passenger seat, trying to find one of my blood pressure pills, and the attendant reached into my truck and turned on the air conditioner to give me a flow of fresh air. Before I left, he asked a friend of his to follow me on a motorcycle to make sure I made it home safely.

Ramona was on her knees praying when I walked in the door. She said she had been praying that I would drive straight home, but I wondered whether she also was praying about whether we should leave Brazil. We had made it through the death threat, but now I was the friend of a murdered man, so I could once again be wearing a target.

I knew that Jack's body would need to be claimed within twenty-four hours, and I also figured that his relatives would be too frightened to go into the street to retrieve it. Part of me wanted to go claim Jack's body for his family, but I didn't consider asking Ramona whether I should go into Castle City to do so. I spent the rest of the day at home so Ramona would know I was safe.

The next morning, I called Jack's cell phone, hoping one of his relatives would take the call. His brother answered and told me he had claimed Jack's body, and I offered to perform the funeral.

Not coincidentally, I'm convinced, I received a phone call a short time later from Ebert. Ebert worked for Member Care, a group of clinical psychologists and counselors focused on missionaries' mental health by helping us deal with the stresses of our jobs. Ramona and I had not been shy about calling Member Care in past instances when we needed someone with whom we could talk through issues, and it had been especially helpful to Ramona during the time when we needed to focus on our marriage. I had to manage stress to prevent it from creating physical problems.

Ebert was passing through Rio and decided to give me a call, completely unaware of the situation we were in. I knew the Holy Spirit had placed my name on Ebert's heart to call. I gave Ebert an overview, and tears began flowing again. Ebert, as the folks at Member Care always did, provided me with wise counsel.

"You need to get your emotions together, and you need to pray," he told me. "You need to think through all of this situation clearly before acting."

I visited Jack's family later that day and agreed to do the funeral. A member of our ministry team was scheduled to sing, and Ramona decided she and the girls would also attend. I thought part of the reason Ramona wanted to go was so she could keep her eyes on me and make sure I didn't do anything stupid. But I knew the main reason was to be there in person to pray for my protection the entire time.

Why was Jack murdered? I didn't know. I heard a few reasons, and I had been asked some questions about Jack. But sometimes, in Rio, someone in Jack's position wound up dead, and we never learned the reason. A few days before Jack was killed, I was told he had become a Christian and announced to the community's leadership that he could no longer murder or plan ambushes to murder because he had "put Jesus in my heart."

I began my message with a familiar theme of mine at funerals.

"In Ecclesiastes, Solomon tells us that there is a time to laugh and a time to cry, and a time to be born and a time to die. Today we are not here to mourn, but we are here to celebrate because Jack accepted Christ into his life. I celebrate Jack's life because he realized there is only one Savior. Jack asked Jesus, our Savior, into his life. His body may be here before us, but he is already in the presence of God."

I paused to look over the mourners. Many were nodding their heads and smiling.

"If my friend Jack could speak, he would say to you, 'Put Jesus in your heart.' Harden not your heart to the voice of the Lord. If God is speaking to you this morning, allow Him to come into your heart."

I intended to attend the burial at the cemetery, but a community official stopped me after the service.

"Pastor, thank you, but it is too dangerous for you to go to the burial site," he said. "You have your wife and your two daughters with you. That guy over there is a friend of Jack's, and he also goes to church. He will say a prayer at the cemetery, and we will bury the body."

Ramona, the girls, and I left the funeral home. I noticed armed men had been posted around the area for protection, causing chill bumps to pop out up and down the center of my back. I instantly decided that if I preached another funeral of a drug dealer or a paramilitary official, my family would not go with me.

Three months later, we closed our ministry's salon in Castle City. Sometimes you need to pull out of a project and move on to the next idea.

However, in addition to Jack, we knew of one other woman who had come to Christ directly as a result of the salon, and we'll probably never know whose lives were changed for eternity indirectly.

Our team continued to minister in Castle City, including me. No further threats developed out of my friendship with Jack. I credit that completely to God's protection.

From my chair time following the death threat and the evidence of God's protection, I came out of this time with a new resolve. Fear would not cause me to want to leave the *favelas*.

But there still would be one more time when I was ready to throw in the towel, and that occasion involved the people closest to me.

My family.

From Ramona's prayer journal:

"Lord, Lord, Lord. Almighty God, I come to you by the blood of Jesus. Thank You for the opportunity to come before Your throne. We need Your help. *Help us, Lord.* Oh, Lord, I need to just pour out my heart before You. This feels like *toooooo* much, Lord, but Your Word says that You will not put more on me than I can hold. So, I come to You. I draw near to You—the only help I know. I look to You, my God, my refuge, a very present help in time of need. Lord, help me to continue to spur Reese on toward love and good deeds. Let me not give up, Father. Let us encourage one another, for You have called us to this place. You will protect, lead, and guide us. I can and will depend on You."

Eric Reese

Chapter 17

Hitting Home

When I attended seminary, I tried to soak up every bit of knowledge I could. My degree plan was set to prepare me to be the most effective sharer of the gospel I could be, and the professors did all they could to make what they taught applicable to what I would encounter in ministry. But, still, there are some things you have to learn that can be taught only through experience.

Such as how to deal with the first demon-possessed person I encountered.

That took place during our first term in Brazil.

The Southern Baptists and the Assemblies of God had the heaviest U.S. missionary presence in the areas where we ministered. Not only were the Assemblies of God missionaries my brothers in Christ, but my brother Clifford was an Assemblies of God pastor back in the States.

When Ramona and I first arrived in Rio, the local Assemblies of God missionaries embraced us. They had established churches and mission points in areas we had targeted for establishing outreaches. I noticed that the residents under the ministry of Assemblies of God missionaries seemed deep in their faith despite, for the large majority, lacking even a basic education. I wanted to learn why those missionaries had been successful, so I began tapping into their hearts and saying, "Teach me how to do this." I was open with the fact that I wasn't out to start a church with them but that our ministry would be starting Baptist churches in areas with an Assemblies of God presence.

As a credit to my Assemblies of God brethren, they welcomed me and shared with me the reasons behind their success. Our denominations had differences in some of our doctrines, but we both believed that salvation comes only through Jesus Christ, the Son of God who came to this earth to atone for the sins of all men. So, while we had our separate churches, there were ways in which we could partner to reach the lost.

Through the years, our relationship with the Assemblies of God missionaries grew into one I considered a beautiful illustration of how representatives of two denominations could work together for the advancement of the kingdom. We were all doing God's work in Rio.

I noticed something interesting in Rio that I would not have expected to take place back in the States: in communities with both a Baptist church and an Assemblies of God church, people went back and forth between the two denominations' churches to attend services. They were that hungry for the hopeful message of God's Word. With both denominations, we were intentional about teaching the doctrines that made us distinct from each other, but the main thing both the Baptists and the Assemblies of God were preaching was that God so loved that world that He gave His only begotten Son so that whosoever believed in Him would not perish, but would have everlasting life.

Amen! (Please grant me grace for Amen-ing myself there, but it had to be done.)

That back and forth between denominations was another example of how ministry was different than in the States. But, again, we learned the necessity of setting aside some of the traditional ways of ministering that we grew up with. That included some of the things that were easy to assume were the correct—and sometimes, thus, only—way things should be done. But the gospel message presented there was the same gospel message that needed to be shared in the States and all over the world. We just had to know our people in Rio and understand the ways that most effectively communicated "Jesus saves!" to them. If the hope-seekers among the urban poor of Rio wanted to attend a Southern Baptist service and then go over to the service at an Assembly of God church, I thought that was awesome. I would much rather both of us reach those people than neither of us reach them.

One way that the Assemblies of God missionaries and we worked together was by sharing our methods for spreading the gospel. My

Assemblies of God brethren liked the structure we brought into Rio from our Southern Baptist training, and I met with them individually and in groups to provide insights into how we set up certain aspects of our ministry.

They, in turn, were happy to share with me certain aspects of their ministries that were strengths from their denomination's training. Because of their charismatic backgrounds, the Assemblies of God missionaries taught me more about spiritual warfare than I learned from anyone else.

And that leads me back to my introduction to demon possession.

Our team had driven up into one of the communities on the outskirts of Rio that requested "the American preacher" come visit. Ramona stayed home with Alicia, and I took Gloria with me.

Typically, when we took an outreach in a community, I hauled in speakers and equipment to show a movie such as the *Jesus* film. We set up our equipment in a park and then drove around the community in my truck, announcing over loudspeakers the time and location for showing the film.

On this occasion, though, we had planned more of a crusade-type setting, so basically speaking, instead of a film.

We had a big turnout that day, with people coming out of homes from seemingly everywhere. With the number of homes and people packed into a *favela*, we could draw a large crowd from a small area. In that crusade, a large number of people said they wanted to commit their lives to God, and we prayed for many people.

After the crusade, we were packing up our equipment when a small group of people came to me and said, "Brother Eric, we have a lady who is demon-possessed. We need you to come pray for her."

My first thought was, *I've read about this. But I don't know what to do.*

I sent Gloria off with our ministry team, and I headed to the house where the lady was located.

If you have never encountered a demon-possessed person, let me assure you, demon possession is real. And it's not something you want to be around if you're not prayed up.

When I arrived, other people were in the room with her, and a big man was firmly holding onto her. Deep down inside, when I came near the lady, I could feel that I was in the presence of evil.

A few of our team members had previously reported encountering demon-possessed people while going house to house for direct evangelism, but this was my first experience.

I didn't know where to start. It came to my mind to ask the lady her name.

"Ma'am, what is your name?"

And she answered, "Ho-ho-ho-ho-ha-ho-ho-ha-ho."

Lord Jesus, protect me! I silently prayed. And I kept praying quietly for guidance on what to do next while the others in the room prayed out loud.

One of the Assemblies of God guys in the room stopped his praying just long enough to tell me, "Don't let the devil embarrass us, Pastor!"

While I was praying, a local pastor showed up at the house. As far as I was concerned, that was the answer to prayer I was looking for!

"What's going on here?" he asked.

"They asked me to come pray for this lady," I said, "and all I've done is ask for her name. So, you go right ahead, Pastor, and I'll go finish loading my equipment."

"No, come on," he said. "We've got to take this thing out right now."

He told me how to pray because pastors have to be able to pray about demon possession in that area.

We went back over to the lady and began praying. I'll admit, I was content with the local pastor leading the way. I was praying, too, but I also was watching what was going on. While we prayed, other people who had been called in joined us and began praying, including some Assemblies of God missionaries.

This went on for forty minutes, and my bald head had to be sweating for at least thirty-eight of them. At that point, I needed to leave to finish up with all the equipment and get my truck. When I completed that task, I returned to the house and arrived to see the lady sitting on the front porch drinking a glass of water. I don't know how it happened, but the people in that room had prayed the demon out of that woman.

When I got home, I e-mailed one of my seminary professors to ask his thoughts on my experience.

He told me I had received a close-up encounter with spiritual warfare and suggested I read up on the subject because I would confront demon possession again.

And I did.

I was witnessing to a transvestite during a Care Night, and after he had shared his story with me, I asked if I could pray for him.

"You can pray," he told me, "but my heart is really hardened."

"I'm going to pray that your heart won't be hardened," I told him.

As I prayed aloud, the transvestite started making noises associated with demon possession.

"I'm just going to hold your hand tight," I told the transvestite, "and I'm just going to keep praying for you."

I kept praying, and the noises kept coming.

Someone on our ministry team hurried over and said, "What's going on?"

"Just pray!" I told him and resumed my praying.

We prayed that the demon would leave the transvestite, and that's what eventually happened! The transvestite settled down and, tired from experience, sat down on the curb.

"Listen," I said. "I don't know what's going on with you, but I know that I'm not here by accident. A God who loves and made the heavens and the earth ordained me to be here. I'm an American, and I don't speak your language great, but God has me here for a reason."

The transvestite burst out in tears, and that once-hardened heart opened to allow us to continue to speak to him about God's love.

The Hex

Macumba is like a mix between voodoo and spiritism in which people call down spirits to possess their bodies. It's very wicked and very evil, and it was prevalent in Rio. I learned that Macumba had its roots in Africa and came to the Southern Hemisphere when slaves were brought from Africa to Brazil.

I once got crossways with a Macumbera (a spiritual leader) who put a hex on me. I laughed it off, but when tragedy struck our family, I had my faith shaken.

Before that, back in January 2003, Ramona had learned she was pregnant. Gloria was almost six at the time, and Alicia was almost three. We hadn't been trying to have another child, but when we got the news, we were excited about our family expanding.

Two months into Ramona's pregnancy, we visited an obstetrician for a sonogram to assess the baby's health and progress. During the examination, we saw the look on the doctor's face that no expecting couple wants to see. The doctor suspected a miscarriage and rushed Ramona to the hospital next door. An hour later, the doctor's suspicions proved correct. Ramona had miscarried.

I could barely get words out of my mouth. We were unprepared for a miscarriage because, with the first two pregnancies, Ramona had not experienced even a hint of a problem and had delivered two beautiful, completely healthy babies.

In a short time, we knew Ramona was pregnant. She had told me she hoped she could give me a boy to go with the two girls. We hadn't learned the baby's gender yet, but I had allowed myself to look forward to the possibility of having a son.

To have our dreams dashed so suddenly and unexpectedly was one of the saddest moments of our lives. I hurt badly, but as I tried to think of what I could say or do to comfort Ramona, I came up with nothing because I couldn't imagine how much deeper and more painful her hurt was as the mother.

My heart broke for my Ramona. She had given so much for our family and me, and I would have done anything within my power to have spared her the pain of the miscarriage. I would see the disappointment and grief on her face and realize how powerless and inadequate I was to do anything about it.

Ramona's faith remained strong in the aftermath of the miscarriage. The Christian life is one of trust and faith, and after watching for years how Ramona had trusted God when He was the source of all our blessings, I gained strength from watching her maintain that trust when life became difficult and confusing.

My first invitation to lead a devotional for the governor's staff came during that time. That phone call was what caused my excitement for the possibility of creating the annual "Jacarepaguá for Jesus" day that eventually came to fruition.

On the heels of the miscarriage, we took that opportunity as an encouragement from God that we were where He wanted us, and were doing what He wanted us to do, and He had larger things in store for us.

Although we hadn't planned the pregnancy that ended in the miscarriage, we had felt such excitement about having a third child that after we were assured Ramona had no medical problems that caused the miscarriage, we decided to try for another baby. I kept thinking back to how strongly Ramona had desired to give me a son, and I determined not to let the miscarriage defeat her or us as a couple.

It didn't take long for Ramona to become pregnant again, and when her pregnancy had progressed to the stage where a sonogram could show the baby's gender, the doctor revealed the outcome: a boy!

We both were thrilled. I love my daughters more than life itself—they're Daddy's princesses and always will be. But I was really looking forward to having another guy in the house. I envisioned us throwing a football around and talking about guy stuff. Considering that I had created the Black Men in Unity club in college to help develop men who lacked a father's presence, more than anything, I looked forward to having my own son who I could lead toward becoming a man of God.

Ramona collected each round of sonogram pictures and placed them in a small photo album to illustrate the baby's development in her womb. We were savoring every moment of the pregnancy, and we decided on a name for our son: Keenan Conrad. My son and I would share a middle name.

While every step with Ramona's pregnancy transpired as hoped, our ministry was doing well too. People were continuing to respond to our evangelistic efforts, and we held successful basic hygiene and medical clinics in the paramilitary *favela* of Castle City.

One day while sharing the gospel, I learned I had raised the ire of a Macumbera by witnessing to a young lady who worked in the woman's shop. I don't remember the exact terms I used, but I basically told the young lady that Macumba was a bunch of trash. To demonstrate my faith in God, I told her, "I don't believe in the Macumbera. I ain't afraid of the Macumbera."

The young lady went back to her place of employment and reported what I had said to her boss, the Macumbera.

My comments angered the shop owner, and she sent word to me that she had placed a hex on me that would cause something terrible would happen to me. I knew that people took curses seriously in Brazil's spiritual culture, but I blew off her warning and didn't even mention it to Ramona. As a Christian, the Holy Spirit lived in me, and I did not believe that any evil spirit could have power over me.

Less than two weeks after the hex had been placed on me, Ramona and I were lying in bed at night. I had been out working all day, and this was our quiet time to talk and catch up at the end of a busy day. Ramona wasn't saying much that night, and we both drifted off to sleep. I hadn't been asleep long when Ramona reached over and shook me.

"Reese, I'm not feeling Keenan bounce around anymore," she said.

Through seven months of pregnancy, Keenan had been an energetic little fellow, and Ramona sensed something was wrong. We hastily arranged for someone to watch Gloria and Alicia, and I hurriedly drove Ramona to the hospital.

By 2 a.m., the hospital staff was running tests. I must have paced my way around the outside of that hospital three times. After Ramona finished the tests, we anxiously awaited the results. Eventually, a technician came into our room and said they had been unable to detect a heartbeat for the baby.

The technician spoke to us in Portuguese, but Ramona asked me in English, "What's he saying? What's he saying?"

Ramona is more adept at Portuguese than I am. I knew she understood what the technician was saying but refusing to believe what she was hearing. I was in disbelief myself.

Ramona was still lying on the examining table, now weeping. The technician must have assumed Ramona didn't understand Portuguese and began explaining what needed to be done. I asked if we could move our conversation to the hallway.

Under Brazilian law, the technician informed me, if an unborn baby reaches a certain age and weight before passing away, he or she must be delivered and buried. Keenan had passed those levels. Once the obstetrician's office opened in the morning, we would have to take Ramona there for a Caesarean section to remove the baby.

I was numbed again, just as I had been earlier that year by the miscarriage. It seemed impossible that we could lose a second baby within the same year.

On the ride home from the hospital, neither of us felt like talking.

We both were going through such horrific pain. I wanted to scream out at God, *Couldn't You have done something to stop this? A curse was put on my life to stop me from sharing* Your *gospel! Doesn't that matter to you? You knew I wanted a son!*

I kept thinking about the Macumbera's hex. I hadn't given it credibility before, but in the heat of the moment, I was angry and confused. With my faith shaken like never before, I began to consider that her curse might have caused my son to die.

Neither of us slept that night. I called the obstetrician's office as soon as it opened in the morning, and they instructed me to take Ramona back to the hospital, and the doctor would meet us there. I also called my missions board leader, who contacted other missionary colleagues to inform them of our loss. Someone from that group arranged for an American nurse to meet us at the hospital. She had come to Rio to do medical work with our missions agency in the slums. Having an English-speaking nurse in the delivery room comforted Ramona when the doctor explained that because Keenan had been so active in the womb, a knot had been tied in the umbilical cord and blocked his blood supply. With no blood, Keenan's food and oxygen supply were cut off.

Our heads were still spinning, and comfort arrived in a flood of supporters coming to the hospital—fellow missionaries from the area and Brazilian friends. Their outpouring of love and support meant a great deal to us.

Our son had to be buried within forty-eight hours, which was the same length of time Ramona was to remain in the hospital following her Caesarean surgery. Once Ramona was released, we would have to drive straight from the hospital to the cemetery to bury Keenan.

I had no idea how to handle all the paperwork and arrangements that had to be taken care of in such a short amount of time, and my secretary and friends stepped in to walk me through the tedious process. I had to acquire from the hospital a written statement with the cause of death. That statement had to be taken to the equivalent of a county clerk's office in the States, where the statement was reviewed, and the death certificate prepared. Once I had obtained the death certificate, I had to go to a funeral home and request a burial for Keenan. Once I had picked out a casket and set the arrangements, I was told the cost and given the option of paying the full amount or making two payments. Then, when the payment was settled, a time was set when the funeral home would take Keenan's body from the morgue. I had to meet the funeral home employee at the morgue to confirm the correct body was being picked up.

The process required a lot of running around—going from this place to the next and then on to the next place—because I was required to be part of every step along the way. And I was very emotional the entire time. While speaking with the clerk at the office where the death certificate was prepared, I was asking questions softly because I was holding back tears. I didn't want to be this big ol' guy breaking down in a public office.

During this process, I confided with a local pastor that despite everything I had preached and demonstrated concerning Macumba, I was questioning whether the Macumbera's hex had played a role in Keenan's death. "You're just weak in your faith right now," the pastor told me. "The Macumberas do not have any power like that."

But, still, I wondered.

Taking care of all the paperwork and arrangements did not allow me any time to grieve. Plus, I was so busy that I didn't feel like I was able to spend the amount of time with Ramona that she needed. Not only had the baby been lost, but she also had to recover from surgery, knowing that she would be going to the cemetery before even returning home.

I checked an exhausted Ramona out of the hospital, and the two of us followed the hearse to the cemetery. Anticipating how Ramona would feel after the surgery, we decided we would bury our son in private, with not even our girls attending.

Alicia wasn't quite two yet and was too young to comprehend what had happened. Gloria, approaching six, described losing her brother as a nightmare. To explain what the doctor had said caused Keenan's death, I showed Gloria a straw and tied it into a knot. That's the only explanation I could give. "God is strong," I told Gloria.

Ramona, I, and the hearse arrived at the cemetery's funeral parlor ahead of the time we had scheduled.

"Is it just you as family members or are there any other guests or friends coming?" the funeral home attendant asked me.

"No, it's just us," I said.

The attendant rang a bell that signaled to employees and others in the building carrying on their business that a funeral was about to begin.

Typically, a casket was removed from the hearse, placed on a cart, and rolled into the parlor. My son's casket was so tiny that I picked it up and carried it in myself.

I had requested the casket remain closed, but Ramona decided she wanted the attendants to open the casket so she could say goodbye to Keenan. I didn't want the casket opened. When Keenan was delivered, I had been struck by how much his features resembled mine. And then I had seen him at the morgue when he was handed over to the funeral home. I tried to talk Ramona out of opening the casket, but when she said she was sure that's what she wanted, I passed along Ramona's wishes to the attendants.

When Ramona leaned over and kissed Keenan on the cheek, it was almost more than I could handle.

I couldn't do anything about it! You know, as a man, I wanted to fix everything. But I couldn't. And I was concerned both about Ramona's medical state and her mental state. I just couldn't fix the problem. I couldn't restore Keenan's heartbeat. I couldn't bring him back to life.

As I watched Ramona looking at our boy for the final time, I prayed, "Lord, give her Your strength. Blessed be the name of the Lord."

When Ramona backed away, and Keenan's casket was closed for good, with only Ramona, me, and the funeral attendant in the room, I began my remarks. I started in my high-volume Blackman's preaching style: "The Lord giveth and the Lord taketh away. Blessed be the name of the Lord."

Ramona sweetly pointed out that she could hear me fine.

I started over with a softer voice.

"Solomon said that there is a time to weep, a time to laugh, a time to be born, and a time to die.[vii] We thank You, God, for the growth of Keenan in the womb. The Bible tells us that some things we will understand later, and we confess to You, God, that we do not understand now. But we still trust in You and firmly look to the days ahead. You said our weeping may endure for a night, but joy cometh in the morning—and in the sweet old by and by, we will understand it."

Through my tears, I could see the tears rolling down Ramona's cheeks. We were doing all we could do at that moment by pouring out our grief to our heavenly Father and declaring our trust in Him.

It was a hot day, and Ramona wasn't in physical condition to go on foot up the mountain to the burial plot, so I walked up there with my son's casket and the attendant. As Keenan's body was committed to the earth, I prepared to head back down the mountain to rejoin Ramona. The attendant, however, recommended I wait to leave.

"You need to stay and watch us bury your son completely," he said.

We didn't think we had paid for a particularly expensive casket, but apparently, for that area, we had. The attendant explained that nice caskets could be stolen with the body still inside, and then the casket would be resold.

As if the entire post-death process hadn't been frustrating enough, now I had to make sure that my son's body wouldn't be stolen for the casket!

I spent thirty or forty minutes on that mountainside while they buried Keenan. I filled the time by bellyaching to God.

"God, I don't understand why this happened, but I can't do this anymore. I can't believe this. You know *everything!* You could have told me what was going to happen. I've always wanted a son, and now my first son is dead. I'm down here reaching people for Christ, and You didn't say anything? And You control everything! I quit. I'm done. I think I'll go back home and be a football coach. I've had a couple of offers to be a coach in Albany, so I think I'll do that. I don't want to be a missionary anymore. I'll be a football coach. I can't believe this. I was so excited. Ramona was seven months pregnant. You are God! I just can't believe this."

In the midst of my angriest moment, I sensed a voice within me gently and understandingly tell me, "I know something about giving up a Son."

When we returned home from the funeral, Ramona laid down to rest. I retreated to my chair.

I stayed in my chair for twelve hours this time. Again, I poured out my heart to God. I told Him all my hurts and pains. I expressed my confusion over how someone who had been called to spread His gospel could be forced to suffer through the death of a son. I wondered how I could end our ministry so we could return to the States for good. I thought about my wife and our daughters and our son, I thought about our dreams for our family, I thought about whether I'd ever want to risk having another dream like that again. I thought about Brazil. I thought about its people and the overwhelming need. I thought about coaching football in Albany.

But throughout my time in the chair, I kept going back to the words that came to me at the gravesite: "I know something about giving up a Son."

I tried to imagine how God would have felt as His Son, Jesus Christ, made His way to the cross. I tried to imagine how He would have felt when His Son said that He felt a separation from the Father. I tried to imagine how God would have felt when His Son asked, "Why have You forsaken Me?"[viii]

The truth is, I couldn't imagine how God felt, but I knew that God knew how I felt. He knew the pain and sorrow I was experiencing. And in my deepest moment of hurt, His Holy Spirit reached down and wrapped His arms around me to lovingly hold and comfort me.

As I wept in my chair, the words of the psalmist in Psalm 30:5 came to mind: "… Weeping may endure for a night, but joy comes in the morning" (NKJV).

In the end, I went back to the call God had placed on my life. Because I had been obedient and faithful to that call, He had protected me many times. And now, as I mourned the death of my son, He was promising to sustain me once more.

Overflow of Comfort

Two weeks later, Pastor Luis Carlos called. Pastor Carlos was my Brazilian mentor.

"I need a favor," he said. He was out of town and asked if I could conduct a funeral for him.

It was the funeral of a two-month-old baby girl who had died of pneumonia.

"No way," I told Luis, to be honest, amazed he even made the request so soon after we had buried Keenan. "I'm just not ready for that yet."

After I hung up, I grappled with an uneasiness from which I could not separate. I didn't feel peace about saying no to Luis. He is a godly, humble, and wise man. He knew what Ramona and I were going through, and he wouldn't have asked me to preach the funeral if he hadn't felt led to by the Lord. I knew the uneasiness wouldn't go away until I had helped my friend, regardless of how I felt and trusted God to give me the strength to get through the funeral. I called Luis back and told him I would handle the baby's funeral.

I met with the family, and it turned out I had to do more than preach the funeral. I also had to lead them through all the paperwork and arrangements I had just trudged through.

At the service, the mother insisted the coffin be opened as Ramona had. The mother fell onto her daughter and kissed her, and wept over her. I felt like I was back in the funeral parlor with Ramona and Keenan.

I preached words of comfort to the grieving family, encouraging them to trust in God and His goodness. The words weren't ministering to only them, though. The words I was saying also were ministering to me, as God poured an overflow of comfort into my heart.

Paul offers an amazing perspective on comfort in 2 Corinthians 1:3-4: "Blessed be the God and Father of our Lord Jesus Christ, the Father of mercies and God of all comfort, who comforts us in all our tribulation, that we may be able to comfort those who are in any trouble, with the comfort with which we ourselves are comforted by God" (NKJV).

Comfort is an endless cycle. God comforts us so we can comfort others with the same comfort we have received. Through my comforting the family, God comforted me all over again. And I believe that the family will share with others the comfort they received from God after the loss of their child.

I later asked Pastor Carlos why he asked me to preach a baby's funeral amid my own suffering.

"Eric," he said in his humble manner, "I knew that if you could preach that baby's funeral, you would be okay and wouldn't fall into depression over your loss. If you could offer comfort to a grieving family, then you would be able to receive comfort as well."

Ramona, however, had become depressed after losing Keenan. For most of the next two months, she stayed to herself in our bedroom.

Most times, when I saw her reading Scripture, I could see her Bible opened to Lamentations. She talked to her mother on the phone quite a bit, and I was glad she had her mother to lean on during that time. But Ramona didn't want to talk to anyone outside of the family.

I kept encouraging Ramona to open up and talk to more people. When I went out to minister, people asked about Ramona. At church, her friends expressed how much they missed seeing her and talking to her.

"'Mona," I told her, "you've gotta talk to someone eventually."

Shortly after that conversation, the phone rang, and I answered. It was Deborah, a sixteen-year-old girl in one of the slums. Ramona had been sharing the gospel with Deborah, but she hadn't chosen to accept Christ.

"I want to speak to Ramona," she said.

I told Ramona it was Deborah, and she took the call.

"I want you to know," Deborah told Ramona, "that I asked Christ into my heart. And I have been baptized, and I'm going to church."

The next day, Deborah came to our house to share more of her story with Ramona. As Deborah unfolded the details, I could see on Ramona's face that she was feeling God's love through the progression of Deborah's story.

The intense pain she had suffered was being replaced by joy, and I knew beyond a shadow of a doubt that, after all, we both were going to be okay.

From Ramona's prayer journal:

@ THE Hospital, all PRAYERS WERE COMPOSED OF LAMENTATIONS (I COULDN'T DO ANYTHING, BUT CRY AND READ HIS WORD... I COULDN'T UTTER A WORD BECAUSE OF THE LOSS AND PAIN I FELT DURING THAT TIME) ... AND I BEGAN TO READ HEBREWS 10 (REMEMBERING MY CALL TO MISSIONS) WHEN I LEFT THE HOSPITAL... I'd go back and forth between the two books for almost two months... God lifted my sadness when I heard from Debora... Hebrews 10 was confirmed... God had shown me that I do have a new child... A new child in the faith and that Brazil is where I need to be....

Eric Reese

Chapter 18

A Final Challenge

"Everything belongs to you—even our two unborn children." Being able to declare those words to God brought a new sense of freedom to our lives. We learned—day by day, tear by tear—that God's gifts and works are always good and that He is always to be trusted. That doesn't mean we didn't grieve. But we grieved with the hope promised in 1 Thessalonians 4:13-14: " But I do not want you to be ignorant, brethren, concerning those who have fallen asleep, lest you sorrow as others who have no hope. For if we believe that Jesus died and rose again, even so God will bring with Him those who sleep in Jesus" (NKJV).

I would do anything to reverse the first miscarriage and Keenan's death, but I also recognized that God worked through our tragedies to bring glory to Him and people into His kingdom.

As a result of the losses our family suffered, I felt much more qualified to minister the grace of God to the people of Rio. I understood, in a small way, how God must have felt when He watched His innocent Son die for me and the rest of mankind. I understood how so many people in the slums had felt when they lost a child. And I also understood how what happened when someone had their faith completely rocked.

The pastor who counseled me regarding Macumba following Keenan's death was correct when he said I was in a time of weakened faith. Under normal circumstances, I would never have allowed those thoughts to enter my mind.

Before Keenan's death, I had not held back in claiming Macumba held no power over the people. After the pastor helped me overcome my doubts, I remained persistent in publicly dismissing the fear of Macumba.

I was preaching one day in the same area where the curse was placed on me, and someone placed a burning candle and a chicken head behind my truck.

"No, Pastor, don't touch it," the people of the church warned me. "It's a hex. It's a curse."

The only fear I felt came from seeing a burning flame near my truck. I wasn't concerned about any kind of hex or curse, but I didn't want my truck to catch on fire!

I kicked away the candle.

"I hate that they just put the chicken head there," I told the people. "I wish they'd left the chicken body. I'd take it home and go cook me some chicken and dumplings!"

I then shared how my faith had been shaken when my unborn son had died. "But no more," I told them. "I want to declare to you, and you go ahead and tell everybody, too, that you cannot say Jesus Christ is Lord and walk around with fear about a Macumbera."

After Keenan's death, I also found myself in a different position: I was the person who needed to be ministered to. God called me to Rio to minister to the people there, but for once, I was the one on the receiving end.

As I tried to work my way through my grief, my secretary would see me crying and ask if she could pray for me. Then she would get on the phone and call other pastors and tell them, "This would be a good time to come visit Pastor Eric." And they would come, minister to, pray for, and comfort me.

Our Brazilian spiritual family poured themselves into our lives in a way that was truly humbling. We felt loved and ministered to as never before by the people we had spent eight years serving. One of the more impactful statements came from a local teenager who told me, "I once heard a great preacher say, 'When life's storms are raging, look not at the storm but how great our God is.'"

"That's right, brother," I told him. I needed the teen's reminder to keep my focus on God, not the storms.

More wise counsel came from a fellow missionary. He and his wife had almost lost a baby girl that was born in Brazil. Their daughter was the same age as Gloria, and they became best friends. After

Keenan died, they gave us a card with a note my friend wrote based on his experience: *"When days get rough and difficult, days that may bring us to tears, we have already answered and responded that we will continue to serve God."*

Those words—I saved the card—continued to speak to me. Ramona and I had decided ahead of time that we would serve God by answering His call on our lives regardless of what might happen.

God's call was greater than our circumstances.

Lucia and Maria

I believe everything I experienced in life was preparation for the work God gave me to do in Rio. By connecting my past and my present as God viewed them, I became less worried about my future. I worried less about what I didn't understand, and I had more faith to trust God for all the things to come.

Sometimes I look back on my life and shake my head. I could have been a statistic—thrown into jail, shot, or killed. But God extended his grace and love to me and took the mistakes of my past and gave me a perspective to share with people who had bound themselves mentally because of their mistakes.

I'm grateful for the people God placed all along my life journey who influenced me away from the racist attitudes which I grew up around, including, unfortunately at times, in the church. As a result of their examples, I came to realize that there is only one dividing line that matters—the cross. People are either saved or lost. Viewing

Willing to Risk it All

people in that manner simplified my life by placing my priority on what is most important to God.

I have introduced you to only a few of the people we came into contact with in Rio. I'd like you to meet two more.

First is Lucia, a Christian we came to know through our ministry.

I entered the *favela* where Lucia lives to share the gospel with the residents. Drugs were stored in that community when the shipment arrived, and I was walking along a dirt road that worked its way through the shanty houses.

Out of nowhere, gunfire broke out from a rival drug gang that had its eyes on taking over the territory. The shooting immediately escalated into an all-out shootout, and I started sprinting to find cover. I heard a bullet scream right past my ear.

I thought I was going to die.

I continued running alongside the road when someone grabbed my arm. It was Lucia, a small grandmother in her early sixties and nowhere near my size. She lived in a small wooden hut that had been built in a ditch next to the road. Lucia yanked me down off the road and sent me rolling toward the bottom of the ditch. With the bullets still flying and before my roll had completely ended, Lucia jumped on top of me.

"I've been here a long time," she said to me. "What you're doing in this community needs to continue. So, if I leave here, I'm okay. But we need you safe."

We crawled into the relative safety of her hut.

Even years later, I could not think about Lucia being willing to take a bullet for me without being moved to tears.

Lucia risking her life for me was a selfless act of love—the same type of love that Christ displayed when He went to the cross and gave His life for us to pay off a debt that none of us could ever pay. It was humbled by Lucia putting her life on the line for me like that—to display that "greater love" that Christ talked about—because she wanted our ministry to continue.

How could I not feel I *must* continue to share God's love with the people of Rio like Lucia?

Maria is the second person I want to introduce to you.

When we came to Rio, we quickly learned precious few churches were interested in reaching the people living in the slums. From a human standpoint, I could understand why. Rio was dangerous. You put your life in jeopardy when you entered the *favelas*. I could see why it was easy for churches to focus their ministry efforts elsewhere.

But God specifically placed the *favelas* on our hearts. He also blessed us with a team of Brazilians who shared our vision for reaching the slums with the gospel.

Maria was one of those vision-sharers.

She was born into a poor family with strong ties to Roman Catholicism, the dominant religion in Brazil. Maria did her best to follow the rules of the church, but at seventeen, she became pregnant. She lived with the baby's father for two years, and the environment was less than ideal for Maria and her daughter. She returned to live in her father's home with her daughter. Maria's sister's family also was living in the same small house.

Needing income, Maria found a job in the music industry arranging events. When her father remarried and moved out of their home, Maria absorbed the responsibility of providing for her daughter and her sister's children. Her situation wasn't that uncommon for the *favelas*.

Maria was exposed to drugs through her job, and wanting to feel like a part of the music community, she soon began experimenting with drugs herself. That led to living as an addict. Paying for her drug addiction on top of the food she was already buying for her daughter, and her sister's children became more and more difficult. Maria chose to sleep on the floor instead of purchasing a bed because she would rather spend her money on drugs.

Although she had been introduced to drugs through her job, Maria lost that job because of her drug addiction. She then took a lower-paying job as a waitress and began stealing the tips left for other waiters and waitresses so she could continue buying drugs.

One day while on drugs, she was working her tables when she came down with a terrible headache. She asked a friend to take her to the hospital. There, her headache became so intense she could not open her eyes or see any light. Breathing became difficult to the point that she felt like she was being choked.

Maria thought she was dying.

That's when she began to recall the conversations about Jesus that her older brother had had with her. Her brother had faithfully shared the gospel message with her for years, and there in that hospital room, those seeds, at last, took root when Maria asked Jesus to forgive her of her sins and take over her life. Immediately, she began to breathe easier, and a complete peace enveloped her.

Maria began attending a church and started reading the New Testament her brother had given her. She refused drugs from her friends, who were shocked she had quit just like that. She also ended relationships with people who would have tempted her to return to her old lifestyle.

I met Maria when I was asked to speak at the church she attended in Canal Vale. During my message, I asked for people in that church to help us reach the lost of their community for Christ. Maria stepped forward to volunteer.

Maria became one of our greatest partners in ministry—one of the Brazilians we have trained to reach other Brazilians. Ramona and I were initially stunned at her enthusiasm for evangelism. But the first time we heard Maria's story of her encounter with God and the way He completely changed her life, we understood why her passion for sharing the gospel exceeded most Christians we know.

Like me, Maria's life story told her that she must make a difference.

Worth the Risk

There were people like Lucia and Maria all throughout Rio. Some we met and helped lead to Christ. God has called us to reach as many of them as possible with the message that He loves them, that He cares for them, and that through His Son Jesus Christ, He has offered them hope for this life and salvation for eternity.

I didn't write this book to recruit more missionaries to come to Rio de Janeiro or even Brazil. As I have described, we had people work with us who quickly learned they were in a place that God had *not* called them to. But the fact is that we are all called to share His gospel, and for the large majority of people, that does not mean moving to another country, to another state, or even to another neighborhood. More than likely, you already are in the place where God has called you to be. And there's likely a Lucia and a Maria where you are, too.

If you are where you are called to be, my question to you, then, is this: Are you sharing the gospel as God has called you to do?

I have offered examples throughout this book of how I have faced and confronted fear. May I now present a challenge to you? The members of the Mount Azul church didn't like my challenge to them at first because they didn't think I had faced the fear they were experiencing. I hadn't faced the exact same fears as their community, but I had faced similar fears many times.

So, perhaps I haven't faced the exact same type of fears you face where you live, but please don't allow that technicality to prevent you from accepting this challenge that I believe God wants all of us to take on.

Here's my challenge: do not be afraid to share the gospel.

I know there is a risk in sharing the gospel. For me, in Rio, sometimes the risk was my life. For you, it might be the risk of losing status at your job, of being ridiculed or called a "Jesus freak" or some other name. Or perhaps even the risk of losing a friendship.

If there were no risk, I wouldn't call this a challenge.

But whatever your risk, do *not* be afraid to share the gospel.

If you know people who need Jesus—and we all do—but you have held back sharing the gospel because of fear, ask God to do two things.

First, ask Him to increase your faith.

Second, ask Him to reveal creative ways to show those people love and compassion.

People may reject the gospel, but nobody turns down love. And once people know that you love them, the message about the God who loves them unconditionally will carry more meaning to them.

We, as Christians, should have the love for those who are lost that compels us to be willing to sacrifice to take the gospel to them, wherever they are and whoever they are.

There *is* risk involved, but the risk is only temporary. What is at stake is eternal.

[i] John 15:13 (NKJV)
[ii] See Romans 5:8
[iii] See Luke 23:39-43
[iv] See Romans 22:22-29
[v] See Isaiah 55:11
[vi] For other examples, see: John 4:34; 6:38; 8:28, 42; 12:49; 14:10; 16:13.
[vii] See Ecclesiastes 3:2, 4
[viii] See Mark 15:34

www.ingramcontent.com/pod-product-compliance
Lightning Source LLC
Chambersburg PA
CBHW071952070526
44583CB00015B/1166